T0098363

RAND

Credible Uses of the Distributed Interactive Simulation (DIS) System

James A. Dewar, Steven C. Bankes,
James S. Hodges, Thomas Lucas,
Desmond K. Saunders-Newton,
Patrick Vye

Prepared for the
United States Army

Arroyo Center

PREFACE

The Distributed Interactive Simulation (DIS) system is an ambitious effort to take advantage of the tools of the information age to help improve the efficiency and effectiveness of the U.S. military services. It involves serious challenges in the areas of technology, interservice coordination, and verification, validation and accreditation (VV&A). The U.S. Army TRADOC Analysis Center (TRAC) has lead responsibility among the services for VV&A of the DIS system. As part of that responsibility, TRAC is sponsoring four efforts aimed at exploring the issues of VV&A of DIS. This report documents one of those four efforts commissioned by the TRAC Director, Mr. Michael Bauman, and is intended to take advantage of previous work done at RAND on exploratory modeling and on validation of models and simulations. The research was conducted in the Force Development and Technology Program of RAND's Arroyo Center, a federally funded research and development center sponsored by the United States Army.

The intent of this work is to develop a framework that encompasses all of the potential uses of the DIS system and illuminates the validation or credibility requirements for each type of use. Because of the breadth of the potential uses of DIS, the resulting framework is general enough to address any military application of models and simulations. As such, it should be useful not only to the DIS community, but to developers, users, and consumers of models and simulations throughout the military services.

CONTENTS

Preface iii

Figures vii

Tables ix

Summary xi

Acknowledgments xix

Chapter One
  INTRODUCTION 1
  Background 1
  Objective and Approach 3

Chapter Two
  TOWARD A FRAMEWORK OF LOGICAL USES FOR DIS . . 5
  A Brief History of DIS 5
  Establishing Credibility and Validity by Logical Use 7

Chapter Three
  CREDIBLE EXPERIENTIAL USES OF DIS 11
  Using DIS as a Stimulus to Induce Standardized
      Proficiencies 13
    Inducing Standardized Proficiencies with Strong
      Transferability 15
    Inducing Standardized Proficiencies with Weak
      Transferability 17
  Using DIS as a Stimulus to Induce Nonstandardized
      Effects 18

Chapter Four
    CREDIBLE ANALYTIC USES OF DIS   21
    Nonpredictive Analytic Uses   22
    Strongly Predictive Analytic Uses   23
    Weakly Predictive Analytic Uses   24
        Stage 1: Selecting a Tentative Argument and Associated
            Hypotheses   27
        Stage 2: Determining the Specific Logical Use of DIS . .   28
        Stage 3: Matching Realism Criteria to DIS Capabilities .   31
        Stage 4: Designing DIS Experiments   32
        Stage 5: Credible Use   34

Chapter Five
    EXPERIMENTS WITH DIS   37
    Design Issues Associated with DIS Experiments   38
        Analysis Issues Associated with the Design of DIS
            Experiments   38
        Difficulties Associated with Big Models   40
    Classes of Experimental Designs   43
        Traditional Designs   43
        Group Screening Designs   45
        Random Perturbations   48
    A Strategy for Designing Experiments with DIS and Other
        Large Models   51
    Dimension Reduction Strategies   57
        Screening for DIS Runs   57
        Hierarchical Analysis   58
        Focusing the DIS Runs   60
    Other DIS Statistical Analysis Issues   62

Chapter Six
    CONCLUSIONS   65
    Typology of Logical Uses and Associated Credibility
        Criteria   65
    Verification, Validation, Accreditation, and Credibility . . .   66
    Implications for the Design of DIS   67

Appendix: SOME NUMERICAL CONSIDERATIONS
    IN EXPERIMENTAL DESIGN   69

Bibliography   71

S.1. Typology of DIS Logical Uses xii
2.1. Typology of Logical Uses of DIS 9
3.1. Typology of Experiential Uses 13
4.1. Typology of Logical Analytic Uses for DIS 22
4.2. Achieving Credible Analysis Based on Weak
Predictivity 28
4.3. Using Experiments to Help Decisionmakers 30
4.4. Matching Realism Criteria to DIS Capabilities 33
4.5. Sampling from the Ensemble of Possible DIS
Experiments 34
5.1. Sequential and Adaptive Grouping of Variables
Screens for Significant Effects 49
5.2. The Sensitivity of the Model Varies with the Size of
the Perturbations 50
5.3. An Iterative Approach, Combined with the Proper
Experimental Designs, Provides a Framework for
Comprehensive DIS-Supported Analysis 61
6.1. Typology of Logical Uses of DIS 66

TABLES

5.1. Partitioning the Model Variables into Classes   54

A.1. Minimum Sample Sizes Required by Design Type to Study a 100-Variable Model, Each Variable Containing Exactly Two Levels   70

Defined broadly, the Distributed Interactive Simulation (DIS) system is an infrastructure for linking simulations, simulators, and live military systems of various types from any of the U.S. military services at multiple locations to create intricate, realistic, virtual "worlds" for the simulation of highly interactive activities. In its most visionary form, DIS would support a complete virtual war, with extremely high realism adequate to support training, exercising, and analysis. Even in more modest forms, DIS represents a potentially revolutionary change in the way the U.S. military conducts its business.

The potential benefits are clear, but there are also risks. In particular, while the list of potential applications of DIS is quite lengthy, a systematic means for evaluating the credibility of proposed applications is clearly needed. In this report we describe an intellectual framework that can be used to structure such an evaluation.[1]

The credibility of DIS (at any stage of its development) cannot be judged for all uses by a single test. Instead, credibility must be determined for each distinct intended use. However, "use" can be understood in many senses and at widely disparate levels. Use can be discussed as broadly as "using DIS to transform the military acquisition system from within" or as narrowly as "using DIS to provide a simulated tank driving experience to trainees." The more narrow the

---

[1]In doing so, we assume that the significant problems that plague current DIS work will, in time, be resolved or greatly mitigated. The utility of such a framework at that time should be manifest, but thinking through these problems now can also help mitigate some of the current problems.

definition of use, the easier it is to identify the criteria for judging its credibility for that use.

The primary thesis of this report is that if use is understood in the sense of the role that DIS is to play in accomplishing larger objectives, then (1) there is a manageable number of such "logical uses," and (2) the criteria for determining the credibility of DIS in each of those uses are generally clear. Figure S.1 presents the logical uses we have identified in this study.

The first division of the tree distinguishes between DIS used as an experiential stimulus and as an analytic aid. The basic question involved in this distinction is, "For whose benefit is the DIS exercise being run?" If it is for the participants, the use is experiential and intended to induce some effect on them. If it is not for the participants, then it is for analysis later, typically by others. The credibility criteria are distinct for these two logical uses.

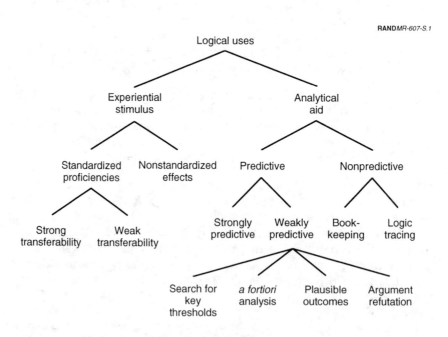

Figure S.1—Typology of DIS Logical Uses

EXPERIENTIAL STIMULUS

Most training, education, and rehearsal uses of DIS will involve DIS in the role of an experiential stimulus. The basic criterion for credibility in this role is whether or not the desired effects have been induced on the participants. To assess the effect, one looks not at the DIS configuration, but at the participants before and after the DIS experience. That is, credibility in this case is determined by assessing the experience of the participants, not by the degree of realism produced by the DIS configuration. This isn't the entire story, however. If the experiential stimulus fails to produce the desired effect, it is important to be able to feed information back to the developers of the stimulus. For this purpose it is useful to further divide experiential uses into those for standardized proficiencies and those for non-standardized effects.

Standardized Proficiencies

Much of Army training up through battalion level is done by training to standards. Using an experiential stimulus, such as DIS, to induce a standardized proficiency implies an ability to measure important aspects of the training experience and to compare the performance with some objective standard. Standardized proficiencies can be found in education, testing, and some mission rehearsals. This ability to measure the efficacy of the DIS experience also gives the developer the ability to measure the effects of added realism or "instructive unrealism" in cases where the experiential stimulus is to be improved.

If the standardized proficiencies have strong transferability (as with, say, tank-driving simulators), then performances can be compared not only with standards but with actual performances in the real world. These cases of DIS experiential use have the strongest objective and measurable credibilities.

Standardized proficiencies with weak transferability (as with larger unit battle-oriented proficiencies) cannot be compared so readily with real-world performance. The correspondence of DIS experiences with real-world experiences is primarily judged by experts, as must be any improvements implemented by developers.

Nonstandardized Effects

Many experiences that DIS might wish to stimulate involve effects that are not reduced to a set of standards (or cannot be). Training above battalion level (e.g., command post exercises), most mission rehearsals, and a variety of other cases fall under this category. Both the ability of the DIS experience to produce desired effects and its correspondence with real-world experiences must be judged by experts. The more that assessment depends on subjective judgments (even of experts), the more difficult it is to ensure that negative training is not taking place in any part of the experience.

Even in this case, where judgments are the primary arbiter of effect, the primary concern is to ensure that the participants are better off after the DIS experience than before. Whether or not this can be done quantitatively is not as important as whether or not an overall positive effect can be discerned, and this is an easier task. It is comparable on the analytic side to discerning whether the improved version of a weapon system is better than the unimproved version. Compare this, for example, with the credibility criteria one would wish if the DIS experiences were to be used to pick the "best" command staff, or even the "best" tank driver.

ANALYTIC AID

Many of the common uses of constructive models and simulations are as analytic aids. In addition, most human-factors research and training after-action reporting schemes fall on the analytic side of the logical uses typology. On this side the primary distinction deals with how predictive the DIS use is intended to be.

Nonpredictive

Use of DIS as a nonpredictive analytic aid places few demands on the "realism" of the DIS system. Bookkeeping uses are often underrated and underconsidered in talking about DIS uses. DIS is functioning as a bookkeeper when it is keeping track of training effects for later analysis, when it is keeping track of timings in a stimulation role for operational test and evaluation, and even when, as in Operation Desert Storm, C^3ISIM was used primarily to acquaint new mission commanders with air traffic information and the military layout. Logic tracing is useful for tracking the consequences of the numerous complex interactions of logistics or operations plans, doctrine, and so forth.

The primary credibility criteria in this area relate to the specific functions. Does the bookkeeper accurately keep the books? Does the logic tracer accurately maintain and propagate the logical interconnections of the system under study? These are more commonly thought of as verification exercises, and, indeed, verification is the primary arbiter of credibility for these logical uses.

Strongly Predictive

We define strongly predictive analysis to be analysis that depends upon the prediction of real-world outcomes with known accuracy. Examples of strong prediction include the use of engineering models that can predict real-world outcomes with very high accuracy, but they also include less well-recognized cases, such as establishing the accuracy of weather forecasters by checking their forecasts against the actual weather outcome over a long period.

The criteria for establishing the credibility of a DIS configuration to make strong predictions are very well understood. To be credible in that role, a number of comparisons of model output with empirical data must have been made, over a sufficiently large set of cases, and a statistical analysis conducted to determine the accuracy of the outputs. Needless to say, even if we presume that DIS will be implemented with very high standards, there is likely to be only a limited number of credible analytic uses of DIS based upon strong prediction.

Weakly Predictive

Detailed prediction of outcomes is often impossible, given the numerous unresolvable uncertainties associated with real combat. Weak predictivity holds in cases where substantial knowledge exists narrowly that—when represented in DIS—can produce behavior that is interesting and apparently "realistic," but where the unresolvable uncertainties preclude credible predictions of real-world behavior.

Many of the (nontraining) desired uses of DIS fall into this difficult category, from operational test and evaluation to force structure analysis, from system requirements definition to mission plan evaluation. It is in this area that we have spent the most effort in trying to establish criteria for credible use.

In this case, the DIS system is better understood as a piece of experimental equipment that provides not answers, but data. Questions are answered by carefully devised research plans that dictate a set of DIS experiments (runs) that compensate for the limitations of both observable conditions and the DIS "instrument" while exploiting DIS capabilities. Credibility of DIS in this role depends not only on the DIS configuration, but crucially on the research plan itself, and credibility is built up through a series of stages:

- Selecting a tentative argument and associated hypotheses
- Determining the specific (weakly predictive) logical use of DIS
- Matching realism criteria to DIS capabilities
- Designing (and running) the DIS experiments

This process culminates—after one or more iterations—in the credible use of a weakly predictive DIS configuration.

In situations permitting only weak predictions, many cases may be plausible, so many model variants and scenarios may be needed to reason cogently. Typically, however, few DIS experiments can be conducted practically, and experimental design techniques are important in order to construct practical DIS experiments. Traditional design of experiments (DOE) techniques, group screening designs, and random perturbation methods can all be adapted to DIS constraints and used to whittle down the typically huge DIS experiment space. These techniques in combination offer the best hope of reducing the experiment space to manageable size and bolstering the credibility of the research design built around the DIS experiments.

CONCLUSIONS

In the past, the credibility of simulation-based applications has been assessed through a process of verification, validation, and accreditation (VV&A). All three of these activities are clearly needed in the context of DIS, but their relative importance varies significantly across the categories of logical use we have developed. For nonpredictive analysis, credibility can be established by means of verification. For strongly predictive analysis and experiential uses that have strongly transferable standardized proficiencies, there are means to validate the system or training protocol, and this validation is necessary and sufficient to establish credible use. For weakly predictive analysis and experiential uses that are either nonstandardized or weakly transferable, subjective judgment is unavoidable in assessing credibility. Consequently, it is for these uses that a formalized process of accreditation is most needed. The reasons for success or failure in this enterprise are, not surprisingly, similar to the reasons for success or failure in VV&A of any model or simulation. One of the things that makes DIS unique is the large number of potential applications of its possible configurations.

We have argued that multiple uses for DIS imply variable requirements for realism and multiple criteria for establishing credibility or validity. Many applications will have individual realism requirements, including purposeful unrealism. The most useful DIS system will be one that allows customization on a per-application basis. It has at times been assumed that DIS will eventually be a seamless virtual battlefield, which will serve a variety of needs. Our approach suggests that the greatest utility of DIS for analysis can only be achieved if it can support a variety of alternative battlefields, including those tailored for a particular study. This suggests that DIS not be thought of as a model; rather, it should be considered a medium that supports modeling, and other uses as well.

ACKNOWLEDGMENTS

Due to the speculative nature of this work, it has been briefed widely before knowledgeable audiences. Each audience invariably adds new insights and nuances, so the contributors to this work are legion. To mention any is to risk unintentionally slighting the many who have added to our understanding. Risk we must, however, to acknowledge the particular contributions of a few colleagues. Mr. Michael Bauman, the director of the TRADOC Analysis Center and sponsor of this work, has been a steadfast champion of this approach. He and Mr. Walter Hollis, Deputy Under Secretary of the Army for Operations Research, have provided guidance and encouragement at several points throughout the project.

Mrs. Annette Ratzenberger, then of TRAC, and Mrs. Sara Tisdel of TRAC provided the important day-to-day liaison work in the formative early stages of the project. Dr. Ruth Willis of the Naval Air Warfare Center (Training Systems Division) and Mr. W. H. Lunceford, Jr., of U.S. Army STRICOM were catalysts for our ideas on training, and RAND colleagues Matthew Lewis and Douglas Merrill were sounding boards and contributors in this area as well. Mr. Carroll Denny of TRAC-WSMR provided data on man-in-the-loop analysis. Professor Brad Efron of Stanford contributed important insights on random perturbations to assess model stability.

The reviews of Robert Kerchner and Bart Bennett have helped us sharpen our focus and bolster our arguments. Mr. Kerchner, in particular, reviewed two different drafts of this work. Hugo Meyer at TRAC also reviewed the draft and made several clarifying suggestions. Paul Davis also suggested several improvements.

With her usual efficiency and good humor, Ms. Laurie Rennie molded the final draft into a presentable document.

Chapter One

INTRODUCTION

BACKGROUND

In the broadest sense, the Distributed Interactive Simulation (DIS) system is an infrastructure for linking simulations, simulators, and live military systems of various types from any of the U.S. military services at multiple locations to create intricate, realistic, virtual "worlds" for the simulation of highly interactive activities. It is a multiyear project and the largest and most ambitious modeling and simulation effort in the Department of Defense. In its most visionary form, DIS would support a complete virtual war that is extremely high in realism, plug-compatible with live military systems, and adequate to support training, exercising, and analysis. Even in its most modest form, DIS represents a potentially revolutionary change in the way the U.S. military conducts its business.

The potential benefits of this revolution are clear, but there are also risks. In particular, while the list of potential applications of DIS is quite lengthy, there is a clear need for a systematic means for evaluating the credibility of proposed applications. In this report we describe an intellectual framework that can be used to structure such an evaluation.

Credibility is strongly related to system validation, and model VV&A (verification, validation, and accreditation) is the primary means used to assess the credibility of application for existing military computer models and simulations. Every letter in "DIS" presents a challenge to validation:

- **Distributed:** heterogeneous simulations at remote locations built for separate purposes
- **Interactive:** large exercises with humans in the loop
- **Simulation:** complex high-resolution simulations with hundreds of variables

Among other things, distributed heterogeneous simulations are difficult to validate because of differences in fidelity and environmental effects between simulations, varying aggregation and semantics for objects between simulations, and different time management and time granularity between simulations.[1] Highly interactive, human-in-the-loop simulations are difficult to validate because human subjectivity, intervening cognitive factors, repeatability problems, and human capability to learn from one trial to the next make stable comparisons virtually impossible. Complex high-resolution simulations complicate matters further because of the combinatorial explosion of variable interactions and the lack of comprehensive understandability, even by experts.

These and other validation problems are being treated by the modeling community through a variety of efforts aimed at understanding validation in general. In addition, the DIS community itself holds semiannual "Standards for the Interoperability of Defense Simulations" workshops in Orlando, Florida, with working groups looking at various aspects of DIS. One of the working groups is dedicated to VV&A of DIS. Complementing the efforts of the VV&A group are two Special Interest Groups (SIG) aimed specifically at the question of credible uses. The "Credible Uses of DIS for Training" SIG is working in conjunction with STRICOM and the University of Central Florida to identify tasks (individual, crew, and unit) that DIS can credibly train.

A "Credible Uses of DIS for Analysis" SIG has also been formed to provide a forum for individuals who are evaluating strengths and weaknesses, developing tools and procedures related to DIS for analysis, and disseminating important findings. Currently in the Army

---

[1]This is, of course, in addition to the difficulties of validating any given model or simulation in its own right.

there is a major test effort aimed at using DIS for analysis. The Anti-Armor Advanced Technology Demonstration (A2ATD) aims to calibrate DIS SAFORs (Semi-Automated FORces) and simulators with accredited constructive simulations such as CASTFOREM and JANUS. The objective is then to conduct analysis using DIS tools.

In addition to these efforts, each service has identified an organization responsible for validation of DIS. In the Army it is the TRADOC Analysis Center (TRAC). Recognizing the complexity of the problem, TRAC has sponsored four separate efforts aimed at the issues of validation of DIS.[2] The work reported on in this document is one of those efforts and is aimed explicitly at a new approach to thinking about validation of a system as complex and problematic as DIS.

OBJECTIVE AND APPROACH

In this report we describe a typology of possible uses for DIS, defining for each category the criteria for assessing credibility. This emphasis on uses is somewhat unusual, but we think it is necessary if effective credibility criteria are to be prescribed for DIS as it is promoted for a wide variety of purposes.

One reason for emphasizing uses is that validation of models and simulations is now defined relative to uses. In the past, validation has been defined as the process of assessing how closely a model or simulation reproduces the real world. However, no model can reproduce reality exactly. This definition of validation traps systems developers in an endless loop. Model outputs are compared with reality and found to be unrealistic in some aspect, feature, or detail. This shortfall can be met by model revisions, but the result will still fall short of absolute reality. The conundrum of when to stop revising plagued the operations research community until the concept of intended use was introduced into the definition of validation. Modern definitions of validation generally follow the one found in DoD Directive 5000.59:

---

[2]The other three are (1) Department of the Army Pamphlet 5-11, *Verification, Validation, and Accreditation of Army Models and Simulation,* July 22, 1993; (2) Robert O. Lewis, *A Paradigm for VV&A of Models and Simulations Used in Distributed Interactive Simulation (DIS) Environments,* 1994, and (3) a DMSO-sponsored VV&A project (IPL #2).

the process of determining the degree to which a model is an accurate representation of the real-world from the perspective of the intended uses of the model.

It is this concept of comparing a model or simulation to the real world *with an intended use in mind* that permits model and simulation validators to break out of the realism loop. If a model or simulation is realistic enough for its intended use, it is valid and validated. Unfortunately, each "use" of a model now tends to become its own special case, and the community is only slightly closer to solving the conundrum in a general way.

Our overall objective has been to improve on this situation. DIS, with its myriad of potential uses, has been an excellent laboratory for our thesis in that it is possible to define general classes of "logical" use, so that

- the role of DIS in any reasonable use would appear in some class, and

- credibility criteria could be identified for each class.

These general classes of "logical" use are groupings of uses into larger categories and the idea of credibility criteria is a generalization of VV&A for each specific class. Chapter Two describes in greater detail the origins of and rationale behind our thesis of logical uses and credibility criteria. The first major division of classes of logical use differentiates between DIS used as an experiential stimulus and DIS used as an analytic aid. Chapter Three discusses the credibility criteria for DIS as an experiential stimulus. Chapter Four discusses credibility criteria for the uses of DIS as an analytic aid.

Although a credible research strategy is important for any use of DIS, a thorough knowledge of that larger strategy was required for identifying the credibility criteria in one of the classes (DIS used as a weakly predictive analytic aid). This issue is discussed in Chapter Four in general terms. Chapter Five discusses the kinds of experimental designs that support credible research strategies and that satisfy the constraints of the DIS system. Chapter Six summarizes the framework of logical uses.

Chapter Two

TOWARD A FRAMEWORK OF LOGICAL USES FOR DIS

A BRIEF HISTORY OF DIS

The concept of DIS arose from ARPA's SIMNET program. SIMNET was a successful effort to use low-fidelity virtual reality (VR) manned simulators as a training tool. Out of this success arose the notion that the approach was useful beyond training in analysis, testing, and operational planning. Early proponents set out to demonstrate the benefit of SIMNET/DIS to planning, analysis, and testing. There were successes and failures.

An early success came during a 1992 analysis effort using the Line-of-Sight Antitank (LOSAT) manned SIMNET simulator at the SIMNET-D facility at Fort Knox.[1] In this effort, by U.S. Army TEXCOM, hypotheses were laid out, an experimental design was formulated, and measures of performance aimed at assessing the effects of different simulator configurations on human performance were identified. A number of samples with randomization were taken, and an assessment was made of the required realism beyond that provided by the SIMNET visual representation. Conclusions were carefully drawn to ensure that unwarranted assertions weren't made that might go beyond the realism capabilities of SIMNET and the experimental setup.

Other tests have not been as successful. At the same SIMNET-D facility at Fort Knox, an analysis was performed for the purpose of assessing the worth of another notional weapon system as emulated by a SIMNET manned simulator. In this case, hypotheses were not de-

---

[1]Smith and West (1992).

veloped and instead the exercise was conducted as "free play." There was no experimental design and only a relatively few runs were made. There was no assessment of the realism provided by the visual representation of the terrain, of the overall environment, or of the physics model of this notional weapon system. Unfortunately, extremely strong conclusions were drawn about the ability of the system to hold X number of hectares of terrain a day in combat.

Similar examples of good and poor uses of SIMNET/DIS are available for training as well. For example, the SIMNET-T facility at Fort Knox is often used to train soldiers at the platoon and company level on vehicle interactions and coordination during a battle. Currently SIMNET has poor realism associated with the terrain: many environmental factors are absent, and all enemy and friendly vehicles have uniquely distinctive colors. However, if the purpose of the simulation is to train soldiers on coordination, interaction, and reporting, these realism factors are not serious distracters. The important criteria needed for training were judged to be the presentation of a reasonable number of enemy vehicles in time and space so that the friendly platoon could coordinate fires and practice reporting; therefore, credible training sessions have been run.

On the other hand, SIMNET has been used in the same facility to train tank gunners on target recognition and engagement. In this case an assessment of the realism criteria would indicate that SIMNET is not a reasonable environment for this. Light levels do not vary, enemy tanks do not hide in hull defilade positions, all enemy tanks are the same color, and the color does not vary as a function of shadows. SIMNET/DIS is a poor medium for this type of training. In fact, a better choice is to conduct this training on Unit Conduct of Fire (UCOFT) simulators that have the necessary fidelity and realism.

In each case the reasons for success or failure can be determined, and not surprisingly, they are similar to the reasons for success or failure of any model or simulation. What makes DIS unique is the large number of potential applications of its possible configurations. Identifying the credible uses of DIS is an encyclopedic chore that demands taking a broader view of validation in general.

ESTABLISHING CREDIBILITY AND VALIDITY BY LOGICAL USE

In 1990, the Military Operations Research Society (MORS) began defining validation as

> the process of determining the degree to which a model is an accurate representation of the real world from the perspective of the intended uses of the model.

The notion that the model's intended use is crucial to establishing the credibility of the model had been in the minds and actions of careful analysts and modelers for some time, so it struck a resonant chord in the modeling and simulation community. Most current definitions of validation now explicitly include the notion of uses.

But what is a use? For any given specific application of a model or simulation, the notion of its particular use is generally clear. If one talks in general about uses, however, a cacophony of possibilities arises. For example, there has been mention of using DIS to "transform the acquisition process from within." Whether or not one agrees that DIS can be used in that way, it is a definition of using DIS for very broad purposes. At another level, there is talk of using DIS for operational test and evaluation, or for training. There is less doubt about the ability of DIS to be used in these ways, but this definition of use is still too broad to inform the validation process of DIS in a meaningful way. At a much more detailed level, one can talk about using DIS as a data-collection device in support of a training exercise. This is a level of use about which there is no doubt. More important, however, at this level of describing the use of DIS, it is relatively clear how to validate DIS for that use: you ensure that it collects and stores the data properly and at the correct times.

It is this last, most operational, level of use that suggests how to identify practical steps for establishing the credibility of a model or simulation. If the use of a model is specified carelessly, it gives little guidance for validation or other quality-assurance activities. But as the example above suggests, if the use of a model is specified in the right way, the sense in which that use can be credible can practically define itself. Is it possible, then, to define a general set of such uses so that (1) all reasonable definitions of DIS use can be found in one or more of these classes, and (2) the credibility criteria of each use are clear?

An earlier RAND report on validation first suggested the feasibility of this approach.[2] The general notion is to define the role that DIS is playing in accomplishing the larger objectives (rather than broad classes of application, which is more common in the modeling community). This is the "logical" use of DIS, and the key is that there is a manageable number of such logical uses. Figure 2.1 shows the logical uses of DIS that we have identified as well as the larger classes into which each falls. The logical uses are the "leaves" of the tree in Figure 2.1. Each will be described in greater detail in the remainder of this report.

We were able to define general credibility criteria in a relatively straightforward way for each logical use in Figure 2.1 except in one category: weakly predictive uses. To describe the validation requirements for this category it is necessary to know more than the logical role that DIS will play; it is necessary to understand the entire research strategy in which DIS is involved in order to establish the credibility of using DIS in that role. That is, one can establish whether or not DIS produces weakly predictive results, but that alone is insufficient to determine if DIS is being used credibly. In all other cases, assuring the credibility of the role DIS is playing is reasonable assurance that DIS can be used credibly. The added complication of weak predictions is the general topic of Chapter Five.

Returning to Figure 2.1, although it is the leaves of the tree that are of ultimate interest, the branches carry most of the logical development. By separating out the logical uses in this way, we have tried to encompass all the reasonable uses of DIS. There is no good way, however, of determining whether we have succeeded. At this point we are comfortable that most reasonable uses of DIS must devolve to one or more of these logical uses, but the jury must still be considered out.

---

[2]Hodges and Dewar (1992).

RAND*MR-607-2.1*

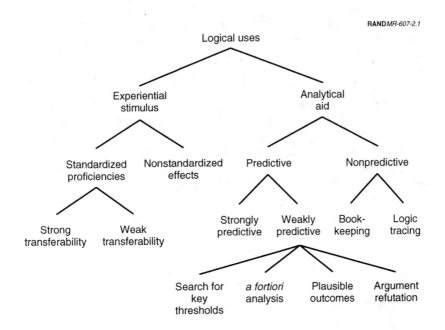

Figure 2.1—Typology of Logical Uses of DIS

The first level of distinction in Figure 2.1 is between DIS being used as an experiential stimulus and as an analytic aid. The distinction is an important and somewhat subtle one. At its core is the question, "For whose benefit is the DIS being run?" In the case of experiential uses it is being run for the benefit of the humans taking part in the run. In the case of analytic uses it is for someone else's benefit.[3] A given DIS exercise can (and not uncommonly will) be run both for the participants and for outsiders, but it is useful to distinguish between the two. For example, a training run is primarily for the benefit of the participants. The logical use here is that as an experiential stimulus, DIS is stimulating the participants to act as though they were, for example, operating actual equipment, and the participants should carry away a training effect from the run. There may also be

---

[3]This experiential-analytic split is somewhat of an "apples and oranges" nature in a logical sense, but it has proved very useful in a practical sense. The proof, then, has been in making the distinction and finding it useful for our purposes.

bookkeeping (classified here as analytic) uses on the part of the trainers to collect information for after-action reports or analysis, but by distinguishing between the two types of uses the credibility concerns are more clearly seen as different and involving distinct approaches. As another example, a DIS run in which subjects are manipulating live equipment in order to test ergonomic efficiencies is most likely to be for the benefit of analysts interested in equipment design. That is, this is a human-factors run whose logical use is analytic, and the subjects are not expected to take away any particular proficiency. Chapter Three will concentrate on experiential logical uses, and Chapter Four will discuss analytic logical uses.

CREDIBLE EXPERIENTIAL USES OF DIS

The primary utility in separating out the experiential uses is that it concentrates attention on the DIS environment's effect on the humans in the loop. Said another way, in experiential uses, the effect that the environment has on the participants is more important than realism per se: "Will the subject experience this as the real thing?" not "Is this like the real thing?" A good example of the distinction can be found in the experiential simulation of acceleration. It is well known that to simulate acceleration for a human subject it is sufficient to simulate the onset of acceleration (by physically accelerating the subject on a motion base for a foot or two) and to couple that with a visual and audio presentation that simulates continued acceleration. The subject will experience continued acceleration in a forward direction while the motion base is literally moving the subject *backward* to its initial position. This is dramatically unlike real acceleration, but it is experienced by the subject as real acceleration— and that is what is important. Furthermore, that experience of acceleration is insensitive to the realism in the visual presentation; it could be as simple as the common computer screen saver that simulates small "stars" rushing out of the screen and past the viewer.

Absolute realism is sufficient, then, but not necessary for acceptable experiential uses of DIS.[1] The fact that the experience is what is

---

[1]Anything short of absolute realism may not even be sufficient for acceptable experiential uses of DIS, in the sense that improving realism but failing to achieve absolute realism may not provide better experiences. For example, an improved tank-driving simulator with computer-reconstructed terrain images failed to improve training,

paramount for these uses significantly complicates the process of developing experiential simulators, but it simplifies the establishment of their credibility. The logical role of a DIS environment used for experiential purposes is to stimulate experiences for the subjects in order to induce a particular proficiency (training, education, or rehearsal).[2] Establishing the credibility of the DIS environment for that logical use rests on testing the participants to see if the proper proficiency was induced. In a strictly logical sense, then, it doesn't matter what DIS does as long as it induces the desired proficiency in the subjects, and this completely describes the credibility criteria for this logical use. This omits a large number of serious issues that plague academics and the developers of training and education simulators; nonetheless, it is only the stimulus itself and its effect that logically concern the validator.

In a more practical sense, it would be nice to expand experiential uses and establish their credibility in a way that aids the designer/developer of the environment as well as the validator. To do that, we must extend the notion of experiential uses to a general discussion of types of experiential use. Figure 3.1 shows two divisions of use below the basic experiential distinction. The first distinguishes proficiencies for which performance standards exist, and the second addresses the transferability of the experiential effects to the real-world experiences they simulate. These distinctions, which will be discussed at greater length below, point to slightly more specific credibility criteria and bridge some of the gap between designing experiential simulators and establishing their credibility.

In many uses of DIS as an experiential stimulus, there will be a variety of standardized proficiencies and nonstandardized effects involved. The distinctions made in this typology emphasize the point

---

apparently because the unrealisms in visual and motion information led to negative training effects. See Padmos (1986).

[2]We will use "proficiency" throughout this chapter to indicate the desired effect that the subject has gained from the experiential use of DIS. This is a generalization, and it includes the "skills" that are commonly the effects desired from training uses as well as the effects desired from education or rehearsal uses. As pointed out by colleague Bart Bennett, this should be thought of in the sense of learning the proper action for a proper stimulus. There are examples of poorly designed experiential stimuli that "tip" the trainee to proper actions in an artificial way. These stimuli induce a misleading and harmful training effect, although they give the appearance of producing proper reactions.

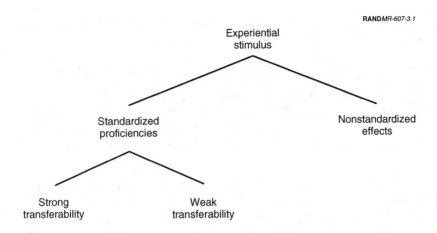

RAND*MR-607-3.1*

Figure 3.1—Typology of Experiential Uses

that there are distinguishable credibility criteria in the separate cases.[3]

USING DIS AS A STIMULUS TO INDUCE STANDARDIZED PROFICIENCIES

Much of the training of individual skills is done by training to standards. That is, an individual is trained and his or her performance is compared with a standard "trained" performance. This ability to measure important aspects of the training experience and to compare the performance with some objective standard is at the heart of what we mean by inducing a standardized proficiency. That is, the training induces proficiencies for which there are standards for comparison. Such standards are commonplace in the Army in individual and collective training up through the battalion level and can be

---

[3]There is ongoing research about the "separability" of complex skills into more simple phenomena and various examples of the dangers of doing this without a deep understanding of the complex skill (see, for example, Sanders (1991)). We will take the general position that if a complex skill *is* separable into more simple phenomena, those simpler tasks can be validated separately. If not, it is the complex skill and its experiential stimulation that must be validated.

found in education, testing, exercises, and rehearsals of all kinds (e.g., military operations, operational tests, etc.).

The key in this case is that establishing the credibility of such a stimulus is greatly simplified. If there are means for measuring performance and for comparing that performance with a standard, the same means can be applied to determine the credibility of the stimulus—the stimulus is credible to the extent that subjects who experience it achieve acceptable results when measured with respect to the standard.

In addition, this case can be coupled with the process of developing the simulator or improving it if it fails to meet credibility criteria. As above, absolute realism is a sufficient but not necessary condition for inducing proficiency. The typical response to the failure of an experiential stimulus is to "increase the realism." In general that is an appropriate response, but it is not the only possible response[4] nor necessarily the *most* appropriate one. Picking the most appropriate response is part of the art of building good experiential stimuli, but in the case of a stimulus for standardized effects, improvement it elicits is measurable and its goal is well defined. If nothing else, this gives the stimulus builder the opportunity to experiment and test until the proper stimulus is created, and it allows both realism and "instructive unrealism" to be varied in the experimentation.[5]

At least two issues still remain in our discussion of the credibility criteria in this case, but a good part of the problem is solved. The first and most tractable of the two issues is defining what level of performance is enough. In general, this will be strongly dependent on the specific experiences and the standards involved. In addition, however, for at least the first few years of DIS operation, experiences will be measured by other standards as well. The performance of a DIS-trained subject will be compared not only with established standards, but also with subject performances induced in other ways. Criteria for establishing the credibility of DIS for that purpose are

---

[4]For an example of a simulator in which a decrease in realism improved the training effect, see Hodges and Dewar (1992), p. 22.

[5]A recent report, for example, describes how training at faster than real time is a particularly effective way of inducing M1A1 tank gunnery skills (see Guckenberger et al. (1993)).

then likely to rest on factors beyond just performance, to include cost, ease of operation, time required, location of simulators, efficiency, and so forth.[6] The ability to measure skills achieved by using DIS as the stimulus can be used in these other calculations as well.

The second issue with credibility criteria has to do with transferability, that is, how well the experience transfers to the real world. Again, in the logical sense of establishing the credibility of an experiential stimulus, this is a moot issue. One should only have to measure subject performances against the appropriate standards. In this sense, the validator is (and logically should be) judging the simulation's credibility based only on performance against the standards and trusting that if the subjects improve their performance against the standards, they will also do better on the real equipment or in the real situation. In more practical terms, the validator of the stimulus should interact with the designer and developer of the stimulus to ensure transferability. In this case it is possible to discuss strong and weak transferability of stimulated experiences.

Inducing Standardized Proficiencies with Strong Transferability

A strongly transferable standardized proficiency is one whose transferability to the real world can be objectively measured. Take the case of a simulator designed to train soldiers to drive a tank. The ability to objectively measure the performance of a trainee both on the simulator *and* while driving a real tank allows one to determine the extent to which the simulator training reduces the need for training in a real tank.[7] Transfer studies of this type are post hoc studies of what happened with a given group of trainees. They do not help much with the development of the simulation. There is another form of establishing credibility of this type, called direct cor-

---

[6]These criteria have more to do with the practicality of using DIS for training, etc., but they are likely to be invoked in discussions of the broader credibility of DIS as a training apparatus.

[7]In the case of driving a tank, just such a transfer study was done and strong positive effects were found in transferring skills from a tank simulation to driving an actual tank. See Sanders (1991), p. 1012.

respondence,[8] that measures the performance of an experienced operator in both the simulator and its real-world counterpart and compares those measurements. To the extent they correspond, the credibility of the simulator is established directly with the real world. To the extent they do not correspond, feedback is available to the developer from expert operators.

In both of these cases, the key is not only the objective measurability of a performance in the DIS environment but the objective measurability of corresponding performances in the rea¹ ¡orld situation being simulated. That is, one can answer—objectively—both the question "Does the subject attain proficiency from the stimulated experience?" as well as the question "If the trainee attains proficiency from the stimulated experience, does that proficiency transfer to the actual experience?"[9]

Using DIS for inducing standardized proficiencies with strong transferability is one of the most credible of DIS uses. The development of the appropriate environment can be tested against clear standards, its ultimate efficacy can be measured directly against the real world it is simulating, and its efficiency can be compared with other means of inducing the same proficiencies. In training, many individual skills can be put into this category. A good example is the rifle marksmanship simulation at the Artificial Intelligence Direct Fire Weapons Test Bed that found virtually no differences in performance trained on the simulator and trained with live-fire weapons.[10] But even collective training tasks found in ARTEP (Army Training and Evaluation Program) tasks up to battalion levels can be included, given that the proficiencies being stimulated can be performed and objectively tested in the real world.

There is a wide variety of educational experiences that can also be put into this category. A particularly good general example is the simulation of classroom teaching by way of computer-aided instruction. A more specific example is the training of air traffic controllers,

---

[8]Ibid.

[9]In this case, the "actual experience" refers to "live training experience." Strictly speaking, it is typically a separate step to ask if live training transfers to combat conditions.

[10]See Torre, Maxey, and Piper (1988).

who depend on a screen in their actual work. There is an increasing trend toward real-world tasks that utilize computer screens, and it is relatively easy to create simulations of these tasks with strong transferability.

Inducing Standardized Proficiencies with Weak Transferability

Not all standards, however, can be so readily compared against the real world. The transferability of many of the ARTEP standards for crew, platoon, and unit-level training cannot be measured objectively. For example, for attack/counterattack by fires for tank and mechanized infantry battalions the ARTEP draws up a general list of requirements which then become the standards against which the units train. But the ability to objectively measure proficiency in the mechanics of attack/counterattack by fires is not the same as the ability to objectively measure the proficiency of the group at that task in real battle. There will be little doubt that a unit can exhibit greater proficiency at the mechanics for attack/counterattack by fires after training than before, and that is the desired induced effect of the experiential stimulus. On the other hand, the desired real-world effect is to have the unit effectively mount an attack/counterattack by fires against an enemy. The effectiveness of those skills in battle is typically testable only against historical experiences and military judgments.

Again, the absence of real-life trials prevents a stronger objective assessment of the transferability of the experiential proficiencies to the real world, but it does not affect the credibility of the use of DIS as an experiential stimulus to induce proficiencies *against standards*.[11] Indeed, the more historical experiences there are of a given proficiency, the more comfortable one can be about the subjective ap-

---

[11] Bart Bennett points out there is still the possibility that wrong stimuli will be presented, or wrong proficiencies developed. That is, no measurement can guarantee that achieving the same standard by two different methods implies that the induced proficiencies are the same. Expert judgment must still be employed here to ensure that the testing against standards means what it appears to mean. There is also the possibility that if wrong standards (or wrong measurements of those standards) are employed, the credibility of DIS will suffer. While true, this is more an indictment of the standards than of the experiential stimulator.

praisal of the transferability of that proficiency. The greatest effect of this weaker assessment of transferability is in the process of feedback to the developers of the experiential stimulus. Any changes that must be made to improve the stimulus can only be described to the developer and assessed subjectively again; each improvement is likely to be judged by a different set of assessors, which opens up the potential for new subjective bias.

USING DIS AS A STIMULUS TO INDUCE NONSTANDARDIZED EFFECTS

Providing an experiential stimulus for nonstandardized or nonstandardizable[12] proficiencies leads to the most subjective credibility criteria of the experiential logical uses. Many experiences that one might wish for DIS to stimulate involve proficiencies that are not reduced to a set of standards (or cannot be). That is, there are many training and educational experiences for which the proficiencies have no objective performance standards. This is more clearly the case in such instances as the rehearsal of a novel mission or rehearsing an operational test on a new system, but it is also the case with many larger collective training and education situations such as large unit training, command post exercises, battle simulation exercises, and situational training exercises.

While it is a goal of the Army to establish standards for as many of the training and education requirements as possible, in certain areas there is a general lack of sufficient data to establish standards. This comes about for a variety of reasons, including the danger of the situation (e.g., training on a nuclear battlefield), the rarity of the experience (e.g., large-scale war), the complexity of the skill (e.g., large-scale maneuver warfare), and temporary inexperience (e.g., with a new weapon system or tactics).

Whatever the cause, an inability to set proficiency standards makes it more difficult to measure the goodness of a DIS experience. This, in turn, makes it difficult to determine the roles that realism and

---

[12]The distinction between the two is somewhat pedantic, but potentially important. For a more careful discussion of an analogous distinction made between unvalidated and unvalidatable, see Hodges and Dewar (1992).

"instructive unrealism" play in producing a good experience. Even so, it is still the effect that the stimulus has on its subjects that matters most.[13] That effect, however, must now be judged subjectively, by experts, either before or after the experience. If before, the expert judges the stimulus by interacting with it and evaluating its potential for providing a good experience. If after, the expert is judging whether the subjects are more proficient than they were before the training.[14]

As with using DIS as an experiential stimulus for standardized proficiencies, just how much "face validity" (as judged by an expert) that must be attained will depend on the specific use. There will be a wide range of credibility levels. At one end of the scale will be uses for which there is little expertise in DIS experiences. In the case of a rehearsal of an unfamiliar and urgent mission, for example, an acceptable level of credibility might be "anything that can be done today and doesn't give negative training is good enough." At the other end of the scale, an embedded training stimulus[15] is likely to be judged very strictly by people with extensive experience on the actual system.

The largest concern in this area is to ensure that no "negative" experiences are induced. In a command post exercise, for example, an ancillary simulation of the effects of a given weapon could leave participants with an erroneous impression of the weapon's effectiveness in an exercise that is otherwise judged to have been acceptable from the standpoint of its command objectives. This is more likely to be

---

[13]This is a very important philosophical distinction. The goal in inducing proficiencies is to produce *better* soldiers. Any training stimulus that avoids negative training effects will do that. At some point there must be concerns for how expensive, how efficient, etc., it is to produce certain gains in soldiering; but in terms of validating the training stimulus, it is sufficient to establish strong reasons to believe that training will take, or has taken, place.

[14]As a point of pedantry, this is not quite the same as an After-Action Report, which is more about educational feedback and grading of performance than about whether or not the subjects got trained during their experience. On the other hand, a good After-Action Report will provide further feedback to the trainees *and* assess the quality of training they received.

[15]An embedded training stimulus is one in which the training is done on actual equipment that is being driven by a training program. An actual air traffic control system being driven by a program that simulates air traffic on the operator's screen is a good example here.

the case in experiential uses without standards against which to compare. There is a variety of methods for dealing with negative ancillary training such as this, but it is important to be more wary of such effects in areas dealing with nonstandardized effects.

In the end, it is still expert judgments that are both necessary and sufficient to validate the use of DIS as a training stimulus for non-standardized experiences. Transferability of those skills to the real-world situations being simulated must also be done judgmentally.

Chapter Four

CREDIBLE ANALYTIC USES OF DIS

In this chapter we describe the analytic side of the typology of logical uses for DIS (see Figure 4.1). For each category in this typology we describe the associated criteria for establishing credibility that are appropriate for uses of that type.

The compelling nature of virtual combat experienced through DIS creates a concern that ill-designed analyses using DIS could be highly misleading. Even carefully done studies could have limited usefulness if, in the absence of clearly defined criteria for credible analysis, users cannot be sure they aren't being deceived by the apparent realism. When compared with analysis using stand-alone (constructive) combat simulations, DIS poses some significant challenges. The use of distributed models (and expertise) creates problems in assuring that the models used are properly configured and in understanding the reasons for particular results. DIS-based exercises involving human players provide the potential of new insights that could not be obtained using previously available techniques. At the same time, however, the use of human subjects creates problems with limited reproducibility, learning effects and other potential sources of bias, and in the reduced ability to explore large numbers of cases.

In this chapter we take a step toward developing credibility criteria that can assist both analysts and consumers of analyses using the DIS environment. The main categories of logical analytic use are labeled strongly predictive, weakly predictive, and nonpredictive.

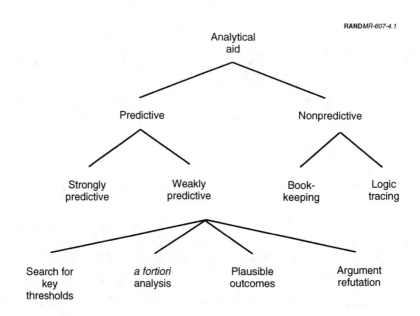

Figure 4.1—Typology of Logical Analytic Uses for DIS

NONPREDICTIVE ANALYTIC USES

Nonpredictive analytic uses are those that place minimal demands on the realism of the DIS system. Applications involving bookkeeping or logic tracing and consistency testing can be supported without requiring the system to predict outcomes. For example, DIS could be used to collect, condense, and display large quantities of information in a role like that of the Air Force C^3ISIM in Operation Desert Storm.[1] This strict definition of bookkeeping excludes even the "bookkeeping" of strategic exchange models in that the data are strictly converted from one form to another without intervening interpretation. Nonetheless, as in the Desert Storm case, this use has its analytic utility. Further, the evaluation of the model is clear:

---

[1]C^3ISIM was intended for very different purposes in Operation Desert Storm, but data input bottlenecks prevented its timely use. On the other hand, its graphical displays were widely used to acquaint new mission commanders with air traffic information and the military layout of the area.

ensure that it reads the right input numbers and then summarizes them without error.[2]

DIS might also be employed to track the *logical* consequences of a set of complex interactions of a battle plan, as in, for example, a logistics feasibility study. Virtually executing a collection of war plans could detect cases where resource constraints make the plans logically inconsistent, for example with two units simultaneously moving down the same road, or a plane being required for two missions simultaneously. As in the bookkeeping example, this is a "prediction" in the trivial sense that it produces a set of logical consequences from a set of inputs, but we consider it nonpredictive because its function is unrelated to the realism of the situation involved. Any realism to the logic must be demonstrated in other ways. The credibility of DIS used in this logic-tracing mode is established by ensuring that the logical consequences are properly derived.

The credibility of nonpredictive uses, then, does not require that DIS predict outcomes or even make reasonable predictions. For this class of uses, credibility follows essentially from verification—ensuring that the bookkeeping function works properly or that the individual logical connections are sound.

STRONGLY PREDICTIVE ANALYTIC USES

Analysis that depends on the prediction of real-world outcomes with known accuracy we call strongly predictive. Examples of strong prediction include the use of engineering models that can predict real-world outcomes with very high accuracy, and weather forecasting, which predicts weather outcomes with known accuracy (even though the accuracy may be far from perfect).[3]

The criteria for establishing the credibility of a model to make predictions of this kind are well understood. In order to determine that a model gives reliable detailed quantitative predictions, a number of

---

[2]A problem that can be tricky in itself, as witnessed in a slightly different venue by the arithmetical computation problems of Intel's Pentium chip.

[3]See Murphy and Winkler (1974) for a good example of the validation of weather forecasting. Briefly, if data show that it rains N percent of the time a forecaster predicts an N percent chance of rain, the forecaster is validated.

comparisons of model output with real data must have been made over a sufficiently large set of cases, and a statistical analysis conducted to determine the accuracy of the model.[4] One "litmus test" for determining whether a model is experimentally validated in this fashion is the availability of variance estimates or "error bars" for model outputs. If error bars from adequately controlled replications are available, then the predictive accuracy of the model has been established. If they are not, the model cannot credibly be used as a predictor of outcomes, as there is no basis to judge whether its predictions are reliable.

There may be special circumstances in which DIS can be used to predict outcomes in the strong sense—for example, in ergonomic experiments. However, as with the vast majority of combat models, for general combat scenarios DIS cannot be experimentally validated because of the inherent uncertainty of future combat scenarios and an insufficiency of data needed for "strong" validation. This is so not necessarily because developers have failed to build good tools, but rather because the nature of the problem does not allow for statistical validation of strong predictivity.

Even if we presume that DIS will be implemented with very high standards, it is likely there will be only a limited number of credible analytic uses of DIS based on strong prediction.

WEAKLY PREDICTIVE ANALYTIC USES

Detailed prediction of outcomes is often impossible, due to the numerous unresolvable uncertainties associated with situations such as combat. In such cases, models of combat may still be useful in a variety of ways. In addition to nonpredictive uses that make no demands on model accuracy, there are credible uses that rely on the model being "realistic" even though it is not strongly predictive. We refer to this class as "weakly predictive" models.

In recent years confusion has arisen between experimental validation of a model's ability to predict system behavior with known sta-

---

[4]See Hodges and Dewar (1992) for a set of criteria for the validatability of strongly predictive models.

tistical accuracy and other means for assuring model quality, which are also being called model validation. As these different meanings of "validation" correspond to different logical uses and have correspondingly different criteria for establishing credibility, it is important for us to distinguish them clearly. This is the reason for the distinction we are making between strong and weak predictivity.

Weak predictivity holds in cases where there is enough knowledge—when represented in a model—to result in model behavior that is interesting and informative, but where too little is known for model outputs to be credible predictions of real-world behavior. Thus, weakly predictive uses are those that require outcomes only to be consistent with all information that is available and seen as salient to the analysis at hand. This requirement is associated with various other terms that are in use generally, including "realism," "structural validity," and "face validity."

It is important to distinguish between a lack of knowledge or data that precludes establishing strong predictivity and stochastic variability in a model that is actually strongly predictive. Monte Carlo techniques can allow the average behavior of stochastically varying phenomena to be strongly predicted. Weak predictivity is not concerned with uncertainty in the stochastic sense, but rather describes the implications for credible model use when strong predictivity has not or cannot be established. That is, weak predictivity deals with situations for which strongly predictive models cannot be established—either deterministically or stochastically.

Nowhere in modeling and simulation is there greater chance for overstatement than when using weakly predictive models. However, it is possible to make useful and credible arguments with them. A DIS experiment that is credible in this weak sense can, for example, generate outcomes that are plausible, and cannot be ruled out. Any time such a model produces an unexpected result (positive or negative), it has created an interesting hypothesis that can (and must) be tested by other means.[5] Similarly, by providing "good stories" that are plausible or realistic, DIS experiments could improve decision-making by improving the intuition of decisionmakers. Here DIS is

---

[5]Typical examples of other means include field tests, exercises, historical research, seminar games, etc.

being used to aid thinking about a problem. Army General Glenn Otis used a combat model based on historical battles to aid his thinking about the possibilities for war in Europe.

The key to credible uses of weakly predictive models is an effective research strategy that explicitly addresses and either resolves or compensates for the uncertainties inherent in the problem of interest. That is, data derived from weakly predictive DIS experiments interpreted in isolation will, in general, be meaningless.[6] The meaningfulness of results in this case depends upon a research methodology that compensates for the DIS system limitations at the same time that it exploits its capabilities. For a weakly predictive analysis to be credible, it must provide assistance in making better decisions. Quite often the decisions, themselves, must be made in the presence of significant uncertainty. The uncertainties that must be addressed in planning an analysis using DIS include not only problem uncertainties such as the circumstances in which future combat may occur or the combat effectiveness of proposed systems, but also uncertainties about the DIS system itself. For example, research strategies must address model inaccuracies, the variability associated with experiments involving human subjects, and the uncertainties associated with configuration management of a distributed system.

How, then, does one establish credibility for analytic uses with weak predictivity? The precise role of the model depends on the research strategy, which varies from problem to problem. Consequently, a single standard for credibility cannot be enunciated for weakly predictive use as one can in the case of strong predictivity. Instead, credible use depends upon the details of individual research strategies, and credibility must be determined on a case-by-case basis. So to the extent that it is reasonable to speak of validation, research strategies must be validated along with the DIS system in the context of that strategy.[7]

---

[6]This statement is meant to emphasize the importance of a context for DIS experiments. As pointed out by Hugo Mayer of TRAC-OAC (private correspondence), "All experimental results contain information. Such information can subsequently be used to advantage, perhaps by pooling. If in no other way, they can provide guidance for the direction to be taken next."

[7]In a sense, each strategy is in effect a different logical use, and consequently the category of weak predictivity contains potentially a large number of logical uses. What

In the remainder of this chapter we describe a framework for constructing a research strategy and fitting the use of DIS to that strategy. In Figure 4.2, this framework is portrayed as a pyramid with "credible use" as a pinnacle that can be achieved only by laying the proper foundation. This foundation consists of four stages that must be successfully navigated in order to support credible analysis. In planning for any particular analysis, some amount of backtracking may be required, as difficulty with a later stage may force one to "slide down the pyramid" and reconsider earlier decisions.

Stage 1: Selecting a Tentative Argument and Associated Hypotheses

Credible reasoning does not require that all uncertainties be eliminated. Instead, arguments for making a decision of interest must be found that are persuasive (i.e., credible) in spite of whatever unresolvable uncertainties there are. Typically, the quest for a credible argument will involve advancing hypotheses and searching for confirming or refuting information. Analysts using DIS in roles where it is weakly predictive face a situation similar to that of experimental scientists working in laboratories. Ill-considered research strategies can result in experiments with misleading or ambiguous results. In general, data derived from the DIS system being used like a laboratory apparatus will be informative only if the experiments are designed to resolve tentative hypotheses or suppositions.[8]

Analyses are generally commissioned because of the need to make a policy decision among some group of choices. A successful analysis is one that produces a compelling argument for making one choice from the available options. At the beginning of an analysis, however, the analysts can generally rough out a variety of arguments that might be workable and support one or another policy choice. Such provisional arguments are either hypotheses themselves, or depend on hypotheses. For example, an analyst might say, "Suppose I can demonstrate that system X will be more effective than Y in all target-rich environments, and that Y will be superior to X only in circum-

---

is critical is not this definitional issue, but rather the procedural question of how to assess credibility, which is our emphasis here.

[8]Serendipitous discoveries do occur, but they cannot be planned for.

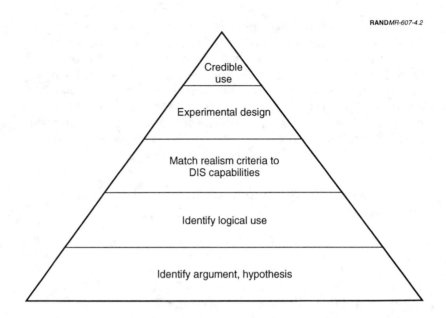

RAND*MR-607-4.2*

Figure 4.2—Achieving Credible Analysis Based on Weak Predictivity

stances that are considered unlikely." The role of the model use is to adjudicate the hypotheses and, through them, the arguments supporting one (or more) of the choices for the policy decision.

Figure 4.3 shows how experiments can be used to help decisionmakers. In the final analysis, experimental results will confirm or refute hypotheses, thus buttressing arguments in support of a decision. Designing a credible analysis requires taking these steps in reverse order. The decision under consideration drives the search for an argument that might be used to support making it. The tentative argument will hinge upon assumptions or hypotheses. Once the crucial hypotheses are determined, it is possible to see how DIS might be used to adjudicate them. This is stage 2.

Stage 2: Determining the Specific Logical Use of DIS

The general category of weak predictivity consists of a large collection of specific research strategies or logical uses. DIS can credibly contribute to a (weakly predictive) analysis only when DIS experiments can be used to refute or substantiate relevant hypotheses. This often will require that the DIS experiments have special properties dictated by the hypothesis under investigation. The property of the DIS experiment that makes it useful for addressing the hypothesis implies the role DIS is to play—that is, the specific logical use for DIS in the analysis. An exhaustive list of admissible logical uses in the weakly predictive category is an impossibility, as creative innovation on the part of analysts cannot be ruled out. Nonetheless, one can at least make a start on a list of general logical uses under the weakly predictive umbrella. The following examples of possible credible logical uses for DIS should help to clarify the nature of the challenge.

Typically, weakly predictive logical uses require that DIS experiments be engineered to have special properties. An example of this sort of logical use is *a fortiori* logic, where cases are chosen to be extremal in the range of key uncertainties so that they are one-sided. For example, when analyzing the performance of a proposed infrared sensor, one might want to perform experiments with no clouds. As clouds will reduce the effectiveness of an infrared sensor, if the sensor proves to be uncompetitive for the case with no clouds, *a fortiori* it will be even worse for more challenging environments.[9] Similarly, in designing a force structure or assessing combat effectiveness, one might choose to examine cases with a "ten-foot-tall" opposing force, reasoning that if these outcomes are acceptable, then acceptable outcomes could also be anticipated for all plausible threats, as they should be less challenging. The credibility of the *a fortiori* argument does not depend upon strong validation of the combat simulation. Instead, a combination of weak validations (i.e., plausibility) of the model, combined with logic and knowledge outside the model (the one-sidedness of the range of plausibility together with the assertion that unexamined cases must bear a particular relation to the extremal case)[10] combine to form a credible argument.

---

[9]Note on the other hand that should the infrared sensor do well for the cloudless case, the experiment would be indecisive and would result in the need to explore further research strategies.

[10]An important aspect of the relations, in general, is that the model outcomes be monotonic in the various input variables. That is, there must be some assurance that the increase in a given parameter will produce a smoothly changing outcome profile. This will ensure that cases outside the extremal bounds could not reverse the results of

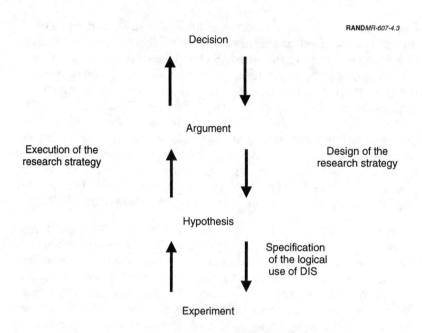

Figure 4.3—Using Experiments to Help Decisionmakers

An alternative to investigating cases that are extremal in input assumptions is to search for cases that are extremal in outcome. For example, consider analytic situations in which risk aversion is appropriate. A possible logical use of weakly predictive models in these situations might be to collect a list of alternative worst-case scenarios and use them to develop hedging strategies or early warning indicators. Note that this use can be credible even though the models involved are not strongly validated and there is no guarantee that all plausible disasters have been identified.

A variety of other strategies for using a weakly predictive model to generate plausible scenarios can be imagined. One might search for plausible best cases, plausible scenarios that refute competing arguments (break stories), or plausible examples that have any other special property that allows them to be used in an argument. Other

---

the extremal cases. For a discussion of the potential for nonmonotonic outcomes in even simple combat models, see Dewar, Gillogly, and Juncosa (1991).

research strategies might involve searching in a space of plausible cases for the threshold between regions where alternative decisions would be favored.

In the context of a given study, the selection of a logical use may involve some amount of search. For example, *a fortiori* logic requires hypothesizing that the results of experiments will support such an argument. Should the results of experiments come out differently, this would require abandoning the attempt to establish an *a fortiori* argument and resuming the search for a credible research strategy.

Stage 3: Matching Realism Criteria to DIS Capabilities

Once the logical use that DIS will play in the analysis has been identified, it must be determined whether the available DIS system can be configured to have the attributes required by that use. This is a question of whether the "realism" of the DIS experimental apparatus is appropriate to the intended use. It is commonly assumed that realism is a single goal that can be pursued by system developers, and that realism can primarily be sought by increasingly adding detail to the system. However, the realism required for credibility may vary with the intended logical use.

One way to understand this is to remember that analytic leverage typically depends upon making appropriate simplifications of the problems being studied. Thus, a particular analytic strategy or logical use will dictate its own unique requirements on the characteristics of the desired DIS experiments. Another way to understand why DIS system properties should vary is to think of DIS as a platform for virtual combat. The power of virtual reality (VR) is not just that it is possible to reproduce the world inside of a machine, but also that particular features of a virtual world can be purposefully unrealistic. In VR, one can be as small as a blood cell or as big as a galaxy. One can play ball in a universe with different laws of gravity. Similarly, much of the analytic leverage from DIS will come from the ability to create virtual battlefields that are purposefully unrealistic in a way that gives analytic leverage. The kind of realism required will vary from use to use, from study to study.

The intended logical use for DIS affects the realism requirements of the system in various different ways.

- The plan of study may *allow* certain kinds of unrealism, which is important, as our systems and models can never be perfect copies of reality. For example, the amount of resolution in any model must be limited. The logical use of a model allows us to abstract away details below some level of resolution.

- Further, the research plan may actually *require* certain kinds of unrealism. The analytic power of particular experiments may hinge on using optimistic or pessimistic scenarios, on dictating that the performance of certain weapon systems be greater or less than anticipated, or on suppressing certain parts of the "physics" of the simulation so that effects of interest can be seen without masking or confusion.

- The plan of research may of course require that some attributes be accurate to a tolerance sufficient for the experimental outcome to be relevant to the question being studied.

Once a logical use is selected, a list of realism criteria can be drafted and compared with system components available in DIS (see Figure 4.4). The result of this comparison could force a re-examination of the plan of research, resulting in the need to select a different research strategy or perhaps to compensate for system inadequacies by other means, such as off-line studies.

Stage 4: Designing DIS Experiments

If one can configure a DIS system capable of supporting the intended logical use, the next step is to design the actual experiments that will be conducted using DIS. When strong predictivity has been established, the ensemble of plausible models is sufficiently constrained that a single "best estimate" model plus error bars can represent the range of possible outcomes. However, with the exception of producing a single plausible outcome for illustrative purposes, a cogent weakly predictive analysis requires consideration of multiple modeling assumptions and scenarios.

Due to the complexity of typical analytic problems, the range of plausible models and scenarios that could be relevant to an analysis will usually be astronomical. The number of experiments that can practically be conducted will nearly always be much less than the

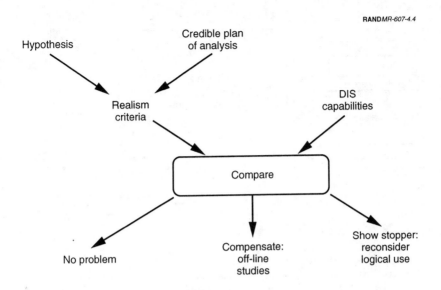

RAND*MR-607-4.4*

Figure 4.4—Matching Realism Criteria to DIS Capabilities

number that could be informative or useful. Thus, one of the challenges of analysis with DIS will be to decide which experiments to actually conduct.

In Figure 4.5 this situation is represented graphically. The hypotheses and assumptions being used for an analysis, together with available data and the constraints of available DIS capabilities, define an ensemble of DIS-based experiments that might be conducted in support of any given analysis. A subset of these will actually be performed. The method of selecting that subset is a major aspect of the research strategy, which is driven by the logical use. This strategy for searching through, or sampling from the ensemble of possible DIS experiments, can be called the "experimental design" for the study.

The specification of a particular DIS experiment involves picking values for a large number of attributes, numeric and nonnumeric. Various strategies may be used to pick these attributes. Some are determined by the logical use, others must be systematically varied to determine the range of plausible outcomes or to facilitate the discovery of salient special cases. The logical use may allow some at-

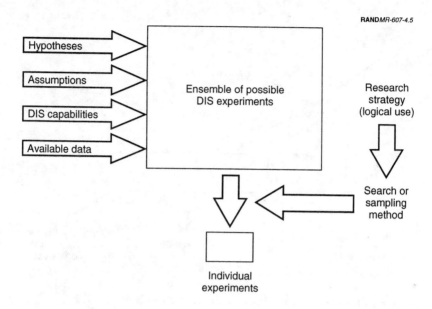

Figure 4.5—Sampling from the Ensemble of Possible DIS Experiments

tributes to be set absolutely (i.e., to an extremal value when using an *a fortiori* argument) or may require the use of adaptive search techniques.

Since typically only a very limited number of man-in-the-loop exercises may be conducted, research strategies that use constructive simulation to examine large numbers of cases to select the experiments to use with human subjects will be a common technique in designing DIS experiments.

The problem of experimental design in the context of DIS is particularly interesting and important for credible analysis. We will discuss this challenge in greater depth in Chapter Five.

Stage 5: Credible Use

Once we have an experimental design, we can finally use DIS as a weakly predictive analysis aid. Credible use still requires adequate means of configuration management and exercise control to assure that the desired DIS experiment is actually conducted. The results of DIS experiments must be scrutinized in order to assure that the results of these experiments do support the argument that was planned. Results from DIS experiments can be evaluated by inspection, by formal statistical techniques, or through visualization. Which of these is an appropriate means for evaluation depends (once again) on the logical use.

Much of the foregoing discussion applies equally well to analysis using combat simulations other than DIS. In particular, recognition of the distinction between weak and strong predictivity is overdue. However, the capability to support live and virtual exercises places special emphasis on DIS as an experimental apparatus, and it makes these issues especially important in the context of DIS. No matter how well crafted the models contained in DIS become, for most applications it will never be credible to regard it as a computational calculator for deducing mathematical truths. If new knowledge is to be reliably discovered with DIS, its role in facilitating *experiments* must be recognized. In that context, the design of experiments becomes especially important. It is to this topic that we turn in the next chapter.

Chapter Five

EXPERIMENTS WITH DIS

This chapter expands upon the brief discussion of designing DIS experiments in Chapter Four. This discussion is related to the analysis of very large models with limited trials, as will typically be the case in DIS-based analysis, but it must also confront the needs for designing experiments with human subjects. The latter need has among its implications a limitation on the number of exercises that can be conducted as part of any given study. Consequently, the question of the number of samples required to make various inferences is also discussed and has important implications for DIS-based analysis. The bottom line is that for many effectiveness analyses there may not be enough DIS samples available to make strong and robust inferences. Therefore, for most analyses, virtual or live DIS runs must complement and/or supplement other, perhaps more traditional, analysis methods—such as constructive simulations (DIS-based or otherwise).

The methods in this chapter begin when the analysis has progressed through the hypothesis generation, logical use, and matching realism steps discussed earlier (see Chapter Four). It is now required that the analysts design the specific cases to be run, that is, select scenarios, parameters, number of cases and replications, and participants for multiple DIS trials.[1] It is implicitly assumed in what follows that

---

[1]For large distributed DIS exercises, this sort of detailed design requires a more mature DIS environment than the present state of the art. Current efforts focus on ensuring technical interoperability between entities. There is only a limited, but growing, capability to analyze the vast distributed outputs of exercises and to ensure that models and virtual entities interoperate coherently. These fundamental issues must

there are stochastic components to the individual trials.[2] The flow of this chapter is as follows: The first section discusses new and exacerbated analytical challenges associated with DIS, with special attention given to difficulties connected with analyzing very large stochastic models. The next three sections define and discuss a design methodology analysts can use, in a reasonable time frame, to help ensure that their results generalize beyond the tiny portion of model space typically covered in studies using large combat models. The final section discusses additional DIS analysis issues.

DESIGN ISSUES ASSOCIATED WITH DIS EXPERIMENTS

The underlying idea of much of what is covered below is that DIS is a radically new technology and how we use it for analysis deserves some reflection. There are elements of DIS that relate to conventional constructive simulations, such as the basic models themselves and semiautomated forces. There are other elements, such as large human-in-the-loop exercises, that are, perhaps, more related to field experiments or anecdotal experiences. This section reviews and discusses some analysis challenges inherent with DIS.

Analysis Issues Associated with the Design of DIS Experiments

Some aspects of DIS address the most difficult analysis issues associated with defense modeling. Examples include: (1) adding humans to the decisionmaking process, a notoriously difficult thing to do well in a constructive model, and (2) facilitating higher resolution in mission- and theater-level modeling through the parallel use of multiple computers and models.

While DIS provides the above analysis advantages, it also poses some new analytic challenges and exacerbates some old ones. These include the following:

---

be addressed before analysts can realistically plan on sensibly altering variables as discussed in this chapter.

[2]Examples of typical stochastic elements in a DIS exercise include human elements in the decision processes and random draws for such events as detections and kills.

- **An extremely large number of potentially causal factors (variables).** By linking multiple simulations together, the DIS environment increases the already formidable tasks associated with analysis and large (combat) models. Some large and well-known models that are, will be, or plan to be DIS compliant are: (1) JANUS, with over 100,000 lines of code, (2) MODSAF, with nearly 500,000 lines of code, (3) Tac Brawler, with 400,000 lines of source code, and (4) the EADTB, with a planned 650,000 lines of source code.[3] For a DIS experiment, with potentially multiple replications of these and other models, linked with several human players, the potential number of causal factors may extend into the thousands.

- **Few trials.** The expense and difficulty of coordinating multiple sites, especially when humans are in the loop, will reduce the number of runs and replications available for most analysis studies.[4] This, combined with the previous concern, will pose a real problem for analysis in effectiveness and other studies. In many cases the number of variables in the analysis will greatly exceed, perhaps by an order of magnitude or more, the number of trials available. This is in addition to the requirements of any stochastic elements that require a number of trials in order to obtain statistical significance.

- **Human elements.** Having humans in the loop adds variability that must be accounted for in analysis. This includes variations among the participants (i.e., random effects modeling in statistical terms) and learning curves.

- **Repeatability and reproducibility.** One of the fundamental principles of experimental design is replication (see Montgomery (1991)). Repeating a stochastic experiment allows one to estimate variability, increases the precision of estimates, and en-

---

[3]Lines of code are being used as a surrogate for the number of variables. Because of a variety of difficulties in defining what a variable is, it is difficult to obtain the number of variables for most models. For example, some elements that are hard-coded may be considered as variables. The counting of local variables, rules sets, and multiple input tables are other examples. Another surrogate for the number of variables can be the size of the input data.

[4]In an Army SIMNET experiment comparing M1A1/M1A2 effectiveness, a total of 16 runs over four scenarios was conducted for each system, as reported in TRAC-WSMR (1993).

hances the statistical power for testing alternatives. Additionally, when tracing causal relations within a constructive simulation, an analyst can exactly reproduce and selectively modify previous runs.[5] This allows one to explicitly identify and test cause-and-effect events internal to a model. It is not clear how this ability to repeat and reproduce experiments can be extended to DIS experiments. Repeatability is difficult if only a small number of replications are possible, and reproducibility is particularly problematic if humans are involved.

- **Known and unknown inaccuracies in the models that constitute a DIS experiment.** All models have limitations, many known by the designers, others still to be discovered through extensive use. The scope of DIS, both geographically and substantively, will greatly exacerbate problems of model management and of users understanding the limitations of their models. Many of the models will have been developed by disparate users for disparate purposes. Developing an understanding of a linked system, including its limitations, requires carefully examining select cases.

Difficulties Associated with Big Models

Live combat is extremely complicated, with a large number of critical interactions. In order to represent some of the most important of these interactions as well as the large number of variables that potentially affect combat outcomes, combat models are often extremely large, sometimes with hundreds of thousands of lines of source code containing many thousands of variables. Of course, a variable is included in a model because someone thought that it could be important in at least some potential model uses, i.e., it is potentially causal. By linking many such models together, DIS experiments may involve significantly more potentially causal variables. The push to add realism into the models, usually accomplished by increasing the resolution, also increases the number of potentially influential variables. Unfortunately, experience tells us that some combat models have regions that can be hypersensitive to small changes in input values, or even chaotic, as Dewar, Gillogly, and

---

[5]All that is required is that one record the initial conditions, including all random number seeds.

Juncosa (1991) demonstrated on a relatively simple Lanchester attrition model. In a more dramatic demonstration of this, the oft-used land combat model VIC was found to vary in Blue tank kills by nearly 100 percent, simply as a function of the precision in a single subroutine.[6]

Using a model in a predictive (strongly or weakly) manner, or simply in an exploratory role, requires varying parameters. In the predictive case one needs to assess the sensitivity and robustness of the model results. During model exploration one develops insights by moving through the model space. Unfortunately, the number of combinations of simultaneously varying parameters grows geometrically. To fully evaluate all the combinations of 100 variables, each taking only two values (100 would correspond to a very small modern combat model), takes 2^{100} runs ($\cong 10^{30}$), not including concerns about Monte Carlo variations. And, as Major General Jasper Welch is quoted in Hoeber (1981), "10^{30} is forever, for 10^{30} is more nanoseconds than have occurred since the beginning of the universe."

To estimate only the 100 main effects in a hundred-variable model, ignoring the interactions that are essential in combat analysis, requires a minimum of 100 runs.[7] A disconcerting fact is that to evaluate the effects of n variables, each taking only two values, at up to

---

[6]See Sandmeyer (1990). This research on VIC (Vector-in-Command) was conducted at the Army Material Systems Analysis Activity (AMSAA). VIC is a large model, with version 1.2 containing over 130,000 lines of SIMSCRIPT code. For a given scenario, AMSAA found that after 12 hours of simulated battle on a VAX computer, 597 Red and 835 Blue tanks were lost. On a CRAY-2, everything else identical, 477 Red and 445 Blue losses occurred. These results are both quantitatively and qualitatively different— providing additional evidence that one should not take too much comfort in the myth that "the absolute numbers are not valid, but the differences are." Sandmeyer (1990) also notes that VIC was highly sensitive to supposedly innocuous ordering of inputs, and finally, that "VIC is not the only (combat) model to exhibit such (butterfly-effect-like) sensitivities."

[7]A main effect is the average change in the outcome (model output) when the variable is set to a different level (i.e., value) with all other variables held constant. Two variables interact if the effect of one variable depends on the value of the other. If an interaction is present it typically makes no sense to talk about the main effects of the variables, for how they influence the outcomes depends on the levels (i.e., values) of the other variables.

m-level interactions[8] in a minimum experimental design requires at least

$$\sum_{i=0}^{m}\binom{n}{i+1}$$

runs, where () is the combinatorial symbol.[9] As a rule of thumb, the minimum number of model runs required to estimate up to m-level interactions is on the order of $n^{(m+1)}$. These bounds on the number of runs required are lower bounds. Monte Carlo considerations usually require that many more runs be computed.

As a result of the large number of runs required to comprehensively explore a model's output surface, and the expense associated with DIS experiments, most current studies with DIS or large constructive models vary only a few variables, the ones of direct interest. That is, of the high-dimensional model outcome space, all the runs are typically taken on a low-dimensional (often only three- or four-dimension) subspace or hyperplane. Of course, the importance of the results is limited if the conclusions drawn from them do not hold true for some distance off of the subspace where the runs were taken.[10] In practice, they are almost always assumed to do so; however, with the sensitivity that combat models often have, analysts should objectively and quantitatively demonstrate that their results generalize.

---

[8]An m-level interaction is the interaction between $m + 1$ variables. Consider the following example of a one-level interaction, i.e., between two variables. Suppose one is evaluating the effects of increasing a system's sensor detection range and weapon engagement range. It may be the case that increasing either subsystem (sensor or weapon) in isolation yields no improvement, in a given scenario, in system performance; however, increasing both systems together dramatically improves the system. In this case the sensor detection range and weapon engagement range interact. Note that whether or not variables interact depends on the portion of model space being studied. Additionally, interactions are common in combat models; indeed, whenever one claims systems are synergistic one is claiming they interact positively.

[9]The combinatorial symbol is defined as $\binom{n}{i} = \dfrac{n!}{(n-i)!i!}$.

[10]To be of value, the conclusions should be invariant to, or qualified with respect to, the uncertainties inherent in many of the variables or reasonable ranges within which the variables may range. In most any combat analysis there are significant uncertainties in variables (such as is typically the case in characterizing the capabilities and strategies of enemy forces).

CLASSES OF EXPERIMENTAL DESIGNS

This section reviews three broad classes of designs; traditional designs, group screening designs, and random perturbations. The emphasis is on what information can be gleaned from the designs, and at what cost in sample sizes required.

Traditional Designs

Models, including the synthesized DIS whole, can be used to help evaluate hypotheses. One method of adjudicating a hypothesis is to perform a formal statistical hypothesis test on variables within a model.[11] For example, one might want to test the hypothesis that in a given scenario system A has greater effectiveness than system B. This is directly credible if the model is strongly predictive or we are making an *a fortiori* argument—pending sensitivity concerns regarding the ability to generalize any conclusions. In such a case we need to estimate the effects of systems A and B, and perhaps some key interactions with other variables, with certain precision. If the number of variables that need to be varied is relatively small, one can efficiently estimate and test for effects using traditional designs.

By "traditional experimental design" we refer to those designs that are contained in the prominent texts and software on design of experiments (DOE). Good references on these include Box and Draper (1987), Cochran and Cox (1957), Kempthorne (1952), Montgomery (1991), and Taguchi (1976). Here we are including Response Surface Methodology (RSM) within the rubric of traditional designs. The range of designs covered by these texts includes the following:

- Comprehensive designs, such as full factorial experiments, which are constructed to be able to estimate all main effects and many interactions, including high-order interactions; that is, those interactions between many variables. The number of samples necessary to conduct a full factorial experiment on a (minimum)

---

[11]Testing the hypothesis within the model must still be related back to a logical use. The fact that a hypothesis is accepted within a model does not necessarily guarantee that the hypothesis translates meaningfully to the real world.

two-level design on 100 variables is $2^{100} + 1$ or approximately 10^{30}.[12]

- Low-resolution[13] designs, such as fractional factorial designs, that are constructed to detect main effects and low-level interactions. A list of many complicated designs, where some variables and interactions are estimable at different levels, can be found in McLean and Anderson (1984). For a design to estimate and test all main effects and all first-order interactions on 100 variables requires a minimum of 5,051 samples.

- Main effects screening designs, such as Plackett-Burman designs and Latin Hypercubes, which are designed only to detect main effects, with the assumption that variables with no main effects are likely not to have interactions—a risky assumption with many defense models.[14] The number of samples necessary to conduct a main effects experiment on a (minimum) two-level design on 100 variables is 101.

All the sample size estimates above are the minimums required to estimate the desired effects. In military models, where significant stochastic effects are essentially always present, many more runs are necessary to have a reasonable probability of detecting smaller effects.

The above designs have been studied and perfected for years. Today's designs provide the most information with the fewest samples. See Atkinson and Fedorov (1989) for more discussion of this and many references on the topic. These designs also tend to be robust to some of the assumptions, such as normality of error. Early applications of these classical designs, and much of the genesis of

---

[12]The "+ 1" is added so that a (minimum) estimate of error also exists. Such an estimate is necessary for any kind of hypothesis test on the significance of the variables.

[13]The resolution of a design is defined as follows: A fractional factorial design is of resolution R if all main effects and interactions up to order k are estimable (k being the largest integer less than $R/2$). To be meaningful it is typically assumed that all interaction effects of order greater than or equal to $R - k$ are zero; for these interactions will be confounded with the main effects and interactions up to order k.

[14]For these designs the interactions are confounded with the main effects, i.e., they can't be distinguished from them. Therefore a strong effect due to an interaction will, without additional investigation, be detected as a main effect.

them, were agricultural experiments. Today these designs, and variations of them, have proven very productive in manufacturing; see Taguchi (1976).

In agricultural, manufacturing, and other areas where these designs are in wide use, the number of factors tends to be small, almost certainly less than 100 variables. Most software packages severely limit (with respect to defense models) the number of variables one can vary, even those designed with defense applications in mind.[15] This limitation may not be suitable for many defense studies, and is part of the reason many defense analysts do not use these methods to study their models.

In sum, the classical design-of-experiment methods are ideal when comprehensively studying or testing hypotheses, internal to a model, on only a few variables, or the main effects and low-level interactions of not "too many" variables. However, the sample sizes necessary for a typical defense simulation, much less a DIS experiment, rule out their exclusive use without some faith that the results are robust and sensibly general.

Group Screening Designs

Credible uses of models, as defined earlier, include discovering plausible scenarios, using plausible outcomes to refute hypotheses, and generating hypotheses. All of these logical uses involve searching a portion of model space to see how outcomes vary with certain variables. An efficient and systematic way of doing this is to use group screening designs. These designs screen for group effects, allowing one to assess many more effects than samples available. These designs are also valuable when performing the comprehensive sensitivity analysis required of many defense models.

A wide variety of applications involve searching or screening multiple items for outcomes that are believed quite rare.[16] One such ex-

---

[15]The package PCRSM (see Meidt and Bauer (1992)) allows up to 39 variables in two-level designs and six variables in three-level designs.

[16]Indeed, if our outcome measures are highly sensitive to multiple variables in the region of model space being examined, it makes little sense to quantify the effects of a

ample, which we will employ as a useful analogy, is the screening of individuals' blood for a rare disease. Such a situation faced Dorfman (1943) in the context of testing large numbers of people for syphilis. Dorfman pooled the blood of a group of men and tested the combined sample for syphilis. If the combined blood tested negative, the one test was all that was needed, with a great savings in money and time.[17] If the test was positive, more tests were necessary, typically using subgroups. Once subgroups were selected the procedure continued until the syphilis status of each individual was known. In this technique the size of the groups and subgroups depends on multiple criteria, including the probability of occurrence of the rare event, cost of the trials, and the number of sequential repetitions available. In general, the lower the probability a variable will be significant,[18] the larger the group sizes should be. Efficiencies are also achieved when there are more cycles to sequentially disaggregate and test significant groups. Sobel and Elashoff (1975) suggest that a good rule of thumb is sequential halving of significant groups. For more on optimal group sizing, and the efficiencies obtained, as well as many more references on the subject, see Kotz and Johnson (1989).

These ideas can be extended to help with exploring and analyzing large models; in particular, when in the region of model space of interest only a few of the variables have a significant effect on the critical outputs. One way in which our problem differs from the syphilis analogy is that here we are using statistics to estimate whether an effect is significant, rather than an exact test. As always is the case, the more replications available, the better this procedure will be at identifying and estimating significant effects. For this approach, sev-

---

single variable, for the outcomes will vary tremendously with small changes in other variables.

[17]Using a simple two-step procedure, i.e., all individuals within a group that test positive are individually retested, Dorfman's procedure reduced the number of tests necessary for determining everyone's syphilis status, assuming 1 percent of the population was positive, by over 80 percent.

[18]Here significant means both statistically significant and practically significant. Statistical significance refers to the observed effect being unlikely to have been that large by chance, with a traditional standard of a 1-in-20 or 1-in-100 chance of getting such an extreme result when none in fact exists. Practical significance is defined as an effect that is large enough to be of interest. It is plausible for a variable (or group of variables) to be statistically significant, but not practically significant. When screening we will usually want to detect variables that are both statistically and practically significant.

eral sets of variables are grouped and then varied together, with each variable taking at least two values. The variables are thus confounded, which means we cannot, without further experimentation, distinguish the effects of the variables from each other; however, we can distinguish group effects—which are composed of the individual variable effects.

In this situation we might not be good at detecting small effects, but we do screen for large effects. Additionally, once a group effect has been detected, we have identified the set of variables responsible—i.e., those variables comprising the significant group.

The size and choice of groupings should not be done haphazardly. The size of the groups depends on the number of runs available, the size of the model, and the analysts' beliefs on the probability that the variables may be significant.[19] The variables must be grouped so that the analyst believes that all the variables in a group will affect the outcome(s) in the same direction; that is, similar changes in the variables will result in similar changes in the output variables.[20] This is done to minimize the chance that two variables in a group, both having significant impacts on the outputs, will cancel each other out, and thus not be detected.

Once the groups are selected, and they need not be of equal size, the groups are most efficiently studied by a traditional, typically main effect design, as discussed in the previous subsection. All of the variables in groups that test insignificant are then assumed not to significantly affect the outcome in the region of interest. More study is necessary for those groups that have a significant effect. A positive effect means that either one or more of the variables in the group and/or their interactions with each other or other groups are significant. In order to determine the specific variables the group(s) must

---

[19]The beliefs being gleaned through the analysts' experience with the model and consultation with area experts. The effectiveness of this approach depends on how well the variables are grouped.

[20]This requires that the experts carefully think how the variables will influence their measures of effectiveness. Through logical reasoning and past experience, the analysts may intuit the direction of the effect of many of the variables. For example, increasing Blue weapon and sensor effectiveness should all improve Blue's performance.

be partitioned into smaller groups and more experiments run. Figure 5.1 illustrates this approach.

In practice, it may not be possible to sequentially disaggregate significant groups, as is illustrated in Figure 5.1. This does not mean that this approach is without merit. In such a situation, group screening is used on those variables that are believed not to be causal. If all of the groups are insignificant, one has quantifiable evidence that the assumptions are valid. If some of the groups are significant, then, the model results must be qualified with respect to the levels of the variables within the significant groups. Additionally, the information can be used as exploratory evidence in future experiments.

Random Perturbations

As discussed above, it is difficult to make general statements about a model's behavior when there are many more variables than samples. For some model uses, some may wish simply to determine if a model's surface is stable in a specified region with respect to several variables. One approach that analysts can use in such a tough situation is to simultaneously and randomly perturb many of these variables and measure how key measures of effectiveness (MOEs) vary. If the MOEs remain relatively stable one has evidence, but not proof, that results generalize in a region (hypercube) of model space around the area of interest.

Even a handful of these runs can be highly informative. The beauty of this approach is that it can be very simple to implement, yet it simultaneously checks large numbers of variables. Its primary drawback is that if the model turns out to be highly sensitive to the perturbations, it can be extremely difficult to track down the specific causal variables and interactions. Thus, this approach can be highly informative if the model is not sensitive to the perturbed variables. This method also provides evidence and insight into the variability of the model when the model is sensitive to the perturbations; however, inefficient information is available on which variables the sensitivity results from—with many variables and interactions confounded in an inefficient design. One can, of course, use the inputs and outputs to get leads on identifying the causal variables and interactions. This information can be used to guide additional model runs.

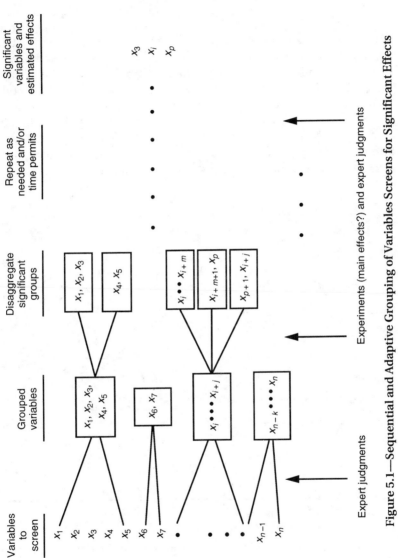

Figure 5.1—Sequential and Adaptive Grouping of Variables Screens for Significant Effects

The number of these perturbation samples and the distributions of the perturbations determine how much can be said about the sensitivity of the model to the large number of uncontrolled variables. Clearly, the more samples the better—though one wouldn't be using this approach if ample samples were feasible. The size of perturbations must be carefully chosen by model and domain experts. One approach is to increase the size of the perturbations until some measure of the model's stability (e.g., the outcome's variance) exceeds a threshold. Figure 5.2 illustrates such an approach. In it, two model MOEs are plotted versus the radius of the perturbations. For small perturbations the MOEs are relatively stable, but as the radius increases, the MOEs start to vary considerably. The analyst can then attempt to track down the causes of the variations, or simply qualify the results to an appropriate subset of model space.

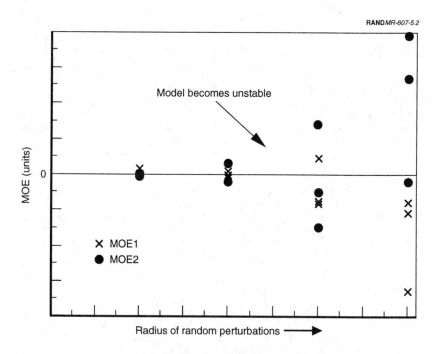

Figure 5.2—The Sensitivity of the Model Varies with the Size of the
Perturbations

For continuous variables one can randomly pick the values between an upper and lower bound, the bounds determined by the modeler and/or expert, depending on the range they wish their results to generalize to, or area to explore. Unfortunately, this requires these bounds to be set for each variable. More simply, one can randomly vary the variables by plus or minus some percentage of the nominal value. While simple, this method may have the effect of moving into infeasible areas of model space, e.g., radar frequencies that are not within a system's capability.

For discrete variables one must decide whether to randomly pick a value among all possible values or in only a subset of possible values. If the values can be ordered in some fashion, one may want to vary only among the nominal value's near neighbors. In any event it is important to try more than one value.

In addition, at times it makes sense to perturb values that are, in fact, fixed, such as the pulse repetition frequency (prf) of a radar. It seems reasonable to argue that since the value is (nearly) constant in the real world, it should also be constant in the model. However, while the variable may be essentially constant, it may be contained in a radar-detection subroutine, for example, in which varying the prf in effect varies the detection range. The detection range is an approximation to what the real value would be and thus should be varied for sensitivity analysis, even if a specific detection range is not explicitly calculated in the model. One can also argue that by their very nature, *a fortiori*, or bounding, arguments do not require one to vary the values of such variables.

A STRATEGY FOR DESIGNING EXPERIMENTS WITH DIS AND OTHER LARGE MODELS

The challenge for analysts will be to set up analysis methodologies that benefit from the enhanced DIS capabilities while abating the above difficulties. In the preceding sections we have reviewed three different statistical approaches that can be used to study models. Each approach addresses a different class of analytic goal, trading off the information that can be gleaned with the number of observations and computational effort required to obtain it. The key is to combine these methods, using the strengths of each, to more effectively study the critical variables, screen for some effects, and ensure that the robustness of the results extends outside the small subspace typically studied. The specifics of how the variables are partitioned will depend on unique aspects of the model, scenario, and logical use, as well as time and budget considerations.

The taxonomy below partitions the variables in the analysis, depending on the study's goals, logical use, and expert opinions, into the following four classes.

- **Critical** variables. These are the variables of the greatest importance, i.e., the ones the analysts expect to have the greatest effects or wish to test formal hypotheses about. These will include the variables being studied, i.e., those that will drive the final conclusions, and those that the experts believe[21] *a priori* will have the greatest impact on the results. For these it is important to be able to estimate the effects and interactions (up to some prespecified levels) with reasonable accuracy. One should use a traditional design to examine these variables. Since a traditional design may require a large number of runs, analysts must craft a research strategy that minimizes the number of variables that get classified as critical.

- **Screen** variables. This is the class of variables to be explored for hypothesis refutation, hypothesis generation, plausible outcomes, or sensitivity analysis. Typically, this class consists of variables that are believed *a priori* to have little or no effect on the results, at least in the region of interest. However, for these variables one wants to be able to screen for large effects, and—in the event that some effects are significant—have identifiable groups of variables that contain the influential variables or interactions. For these variables and interactions one should consider using a screening design. By employing a design that crosses the screen and critical variables, one can also estimate some of their interactions; this is discussed below.

- **Perturb** variables. These variables are those that our research strategy requires we establish some estimate of the model's sta-

---

[21]These beliefs may be founded on theory, previous experience, or simply intuition.

bility to, often for sensitivity analysis. They usually consist of variables that are believed *a priori* to have little or no effect on the results; however, one wants to demonstrate this. These variables will be randomly and simultaneously perturbed.

- **"Fixed"** variables. This class contains variables that will remain fixed during the analysis. These variables are those the analyst believes are unimportant in the region of interest, or are fixed as part of the credible use of the model, such as *a fortiori* arguments, and/or are held constant for theoretical reasons throughout. In current practice, this class contains all but a few of the variables. Model runs will provide no information on the effect that varying these values in these regions of model space might have had on the measures of interest or the critical variables.

Table 5.1 summarizes how this approach classifies the factors (variables) in an experiment.

The designs recommended in this table provide the means for studying effects within the classes of variables. It remains to be resolved as to how to get information on effects between the classes of variables, such as possible interactions between the screen and critical variables—as would be of interest in sensitivity analysis. If the analysts believe strongly that the screen variables will *not* interact with the critical variables, then they can study the screen variables independently from the critical variables, i.e., at one level of the critical variables; otherwise the design should be crossed. A crossed design is one in which all the levels of the critical design are observed at all the levels of the screen design. The benefit from not having to use a crossed design is that the number of required trials for combining the designs is additive, rather than multiplicative.[22] Assuming interactions do not exist is a very strong assumption to make with most combat models. Of course, one can have a design where some of the groups of screen variables are crossed with the critical variables and others are not.

_____

[22]This is best illustrated by a simple example. Consider an experiment with two factors containing A and B levels, respectively. It takes $A + B + 1$ observations to estimate the effects when no interactions are assumed, while it takes $A \times B + 1$ observations to estimate all the effects if interactions are present. For more on this, see Montgomery (1991).

Table 5.1

Partitioning the Model Variables into Classes

Factor Class	Criteria for Inclusion[a]	What Is Estimable?	Recommended Design
Critical	Factors being estimated or tested, or results are believed highly dependent on	Main effects and varying levels of interactions	Traditional, such as high-resolution factorial design
Screen	Factors being screened for effects	Group effects, perhaps crossed with critical variables	Low-resolution group screening designs
Perturb	Factors believed to be insignificant in the area of interest or general stability being assessed	General stability of outputs to perturbations in the area of interest	Randomly generated cases
Fixed	Known not to influence outputs or are theoretically or logically fixed	Nothing	Not applicable

[a]The table gives very broad criteria for inclusion in a class. The actual detailed criteria depend on the logical use for estimating or testing for effects. This can range from formal hypothesis testing to exploring plausible outcomes—as was discussed in the preceding sections.

One also must decide whether to "randomly shake" the perturb variables at a fixed level of the critical and screen variables. Again, if only the effects of the variables to be perturbed are of interest, it is unnecessary to simultaneously vary them with the other variables. If one is concerned about potential interactions, the perturbations must be made for at least a couple of settings of the other variables. If the perturb variables design is crossed with the other variables design, then one interpretation is that each level of the perturb variables is a block (see Montgomery (1991) for more on blocking).

In an effort to provide some guidance as to the cost in samples required for the combined design, we provide here an illustrative equation that quantifies the number of samples with respect to a combined design. This equation is highly stylized, with many unrealistic assumptions, such as a constant number of levels for each variable. However, it provides a feel for the consequences of adding variables, modifying the number of levels, and changing the resolution. The equation also does not include samples for replication or estimating error. The minimum number of samples needed can be very roughly approximated by

$$\text{Samples} \cong \sum_{i=0}^{I_C} \binom{N_C}{i+1}(C-1)^{i+1} \oplus \sum_{j=0}^{I_S} \binom{N_S/G}{j+1}(D-1)^{j+1} + P,$$

where

$\oplus$ = $\times$ if critical design is crossed with screen design, + otherwise,

N_C = number of critical variables,

C = number of levels for each critical variable,[23]

I_C = highest level of interaction, with I_C corresponding to the interaction of $I_C + 1$ variables, that the critical design is able to estimate or confound with higher-level interactions,[24]

N_S = number of screen variables,

G = number of variables in a group,[25]

D = number of levels for each screening group; this will typically be two,

I_S = Highest level of group interaction that the screen design is able to estimate or confound with higher-level interactions,

P = number of perturbations.

Some key points to note from the equation: there are high costs in samples required for increasing the number of variables in the critical class (N_C), increasing the number of levels (C, D), and increasing

---

[23]In practice the number of levels of variable will not be the same.

[24]The design can be defined so that differing levels of interactions are estimable (or confounded with high-level interactions) for different sets of variables.

[25]The groups need not be of equal size in practice.

the interactions to estimate (I_C, I_S). Potential methods to reduce the number of samples required include

- Moving as many variables as possible into the fixed, screen, and perturb classes, respectively,

- Limiting the number of interactions to estimate,

- Reducing the levels of the variables varied,[26]

- Increasing the size of the groups (G) in screen variables, and

- Not crossing the critical and screen designs.

Of course, all of these result in some loss of information. See the appendix for an example of the costs and benefits of several options within this framework.

When implementing such a procedure one must choose the levels of the variables. These choices must be supported by domain and model experts. The selections will be highly dependent on the analysis goals, scenarios, and logical use. In general, the variation in the variables determines the volume of model space about which one can make inferences. The number of replications, varying by class of variable, will determine the ability to detect differences in outcomes.

Where possible, one should use a continuous MOE (like kill or loss rates) rather than dichotomous outcomes, such as win-lose. The reasoning behind this is that it often takes far too many observations to get reasonable statistical power for dichotomous outcomes.[27] Another approach to increase the ability to detect effects is to look at process measures, rather than simply outcome measures. For example, the series of pairwise detections within a simulation may provide thousands of data points for analysis, compared to a single outcome measure such as win-lose or exchange ratio. Still, for many

---

[26]Reducing the number of levels reduces the ability to estimate more complex relationships. For example, if a quantitative variable has only two levels, one can fit only a linear relationship to the response as a function of the variable. Three levels allows one to fit quadratics (i.e., curves).

[27]To ensure that there is a 95 percent chance of statistically detecting a 10 percent difference in dichotomous outcomes, for only two inputs, requires about 200 runs.

fine inferences the sample sizes required for formal statistical testing will typically not be available in studies using DIS exclusively.

DIMENSION REDUCTION STRATEGIES

The preceding sections demonstrate that the dimensionality of large combat models poses severe analysis difficulties. One way to abate these difficulties is to reduce the dimension of model space that needs to be explored in support of the logical use.

A common belief in most model applications is that in the area of interest only a few variables heavily influence outcomes. If this is not true, the models are extremely difficult to understand and too unstable to draw firm or generalizable conclusions from. Two approaches that can be used to reduce the dimensions of the space to be examined in a DIS-supported analysis are (1) carefully use previous analysis, experts' opinions, and constructive simulation experimentation (essentially screening) to push variables into classes requiring fewer DIS samples to study, and (2) use hierarchical analysis and modeling. These approaches should be used aggressively and in combination, where possible, in an attempt to dramatically reduce the number of samples required from the DIS portion of the analysis—including robustness and sensitivity analysis. Essentially, for macro outcomes,[28] the DIS portion can be used, credibly, only to inform and support other results or to generate hypotheses that need to be evaluated elsewhere.

Screening for DIS Runs

Typically, the DIS portion of an analysis will involve very few trials. The human element of DIS, i.e., the interactive part, adds much to the expense and reproducibility difficulties associated with DIS experiments. When it is removed from the system, one can take many

---

[28]Macro outcomes are those where only one observation is available from a given run, such as battle exchange ratios or win-lose determinations. For process-level outcomes, such as detections and engagements, there may be thousands of observations within a single DIS run.

more runs and precise replications.[29] Therefore, before doing a DIS analysis using humans, it makes sense to perform extensive exploratory and screening runs with constructive simulations—this, of course, requires using constructive forces (and possibly some SAFORs (semiautomated forces)) as surrogates for the humans. This screening can be efficiently accomplished via the methods discussed in the previous sections. The screening will identify the variables that influence the results and the human-factors variables (from among those identified by other means) that are important in determining outcomes. This, combined with previous experience and experts' opinions, should enable one to reduce the number of variables that need to be systematically varied.[30]

Another benefit of this approach is that it may identify some of the critical decisionmaking entities. In an analysis that contains both humans and constructive decisionmakers, the analyst may wish to weigh the assignment of people to the critical entities—as opposed to a simple random assignment of people to entities.

Hierarchical Analysis

The principle behind hierarchical analysis, as we define explicitly below, is to model explicitly, wherever possible, only those variables that are of interest or to which the output measures are sensitive. In practice this is impossible with most current combat models, which typically have limited flexibility in resolution. Over time the resolutions of such models tend to grow as the models are "improved." The high level of resolution encumbers all subsequent analyses with the model, making it hard to trace causal links and impossible to perform comprehensive sensitivity analysis.

The variables of interest may be known *a priori*; however, it is not likely that all the variables that may be causal will be known in advance—though some of them probably can be intuited. Thus, the analyst has a chicken-and-egg problem. One wants to explicitly

---

[29]When not interacting with humans, the models can be run in parallel, at faster than real time, 24 hours a day.

[30]Using information between studies requires systematic recording of the scenarios and critical variables.

model only those variables upon which outputs vary; but these are not necessarily known in advance of the analysis. A hierarchical approach initially models objects and processes at the highest possible aggregate level. The objects and processes are disaggregated only if they are of interest and/or significantly impact the MOEs. Since DIS experiments are so valuable, one will typically attempt most of this with the constructive models portion of the analysis.

The following example may help illustrate what so far has been very abstract. Consider the radar detection functions in a mission-level combat model. At a first cut the radars might be modeled by simple cookie-cutters. If the results are sensitive to the range at which objects are detected, the simple radar cookie-cutter might be adjusted to account for beam patterns and target radar cross sections. If the results are still sensitive to this characterization, the model can be further decomposed with radar range equations within the beam patterns. The successive disaggregations would continue, with constructive models, until the outputs were relatively insensitive to moderate changes in the variables that compose the detection process. Hopefully, this would terminate before a time consuming ray-tracing model with site-specific clutter is required.

In the previous paragraph it is implicitly assumed that successive disaggregations are relatively smooth. This may hold if the models are designed to be integrated hierarchical variable-resolution. In such a case the inputs of the lower level of resolution are the outputs of the next-higher level of resolution. This is extremely difficult to do in practice. The common approach is to have alternate submodels. One hopes that, if the results are insensitive to changes in a low-resolution model, they will also be in a high-resolution model (though if they are not integrated, there is no guarantee of this).

We have touched on just some of the basic ideas in hierarchical modeling. They can be very complex and quite subtle.[31] The method of sequential hierarchical analysis is typically not available when using combat models. Most models have fixed, or nearly fixed, resolution. To do the above analysis requires models to be built that

---

[31]For more on this, readers are encouraged to see Davis and Huber (1992) and Davis and Hillestad (1993).

facilitate, where possible, such a sequential hierarchical analysis. The benefits of doing so will be analyses that are more transparent and have dramatically improved sensitivity analysis.

Focusing the DIS Runs

The upshot of the two approaches above, screening and hierarchical models, is that samples with humans and/or multiple disparate sites are extremely valuable. Concerted efforts should thus be taken with constructive simulations and expert opinions, both before and concurrent with full-on interactive DIS experiments, to dramatically reduce the number of variables that need to be studied with DIS. Figure 5.3 illustrates how one combines the dimensional reduction strategies with the experimental designs in a comprehensive DIS-supported analysis.

The figure shows how one uses the DIS portion of the analysis in a small volume of model space. Starting with the unmanageable feasible model space, by identifying the "logical use" one may eliminate much of the space it will be necessary to explore. An example is an *a fortiori* use, which requires that only boundary cases be run. Using expert knowledge, perhaps gleaned from previous, related, analysis efforts, one can further reduce the amount of space one needs to study. Once an area of interest has been established, the analysis continues with, if they are available, hierarchical methods and exploratory designs. These designs will likely consist mostly of the group screening and main effect designs. These runs will identify the key variables in the area of interest, i.e., the critical portion of model space will have been identified. Extensive constructive-based runs can then be made, using a mixture of the designs discussed above. These runs can then be used to guide the design for the interactive DIS runs. Since, in all likelihood, only a few full-on DIS runs will be available, only those areas of highest interest and that are integrally linked to human perception and decisionmaking will be used.

It may be that the DIS portion of the analysis is only used to support or inform some external, say constructive-based, analysis, or perhaps used primarily to generate potential hypotheses and questions to be analyzed elsewhere. An example of using DIS to support construc-

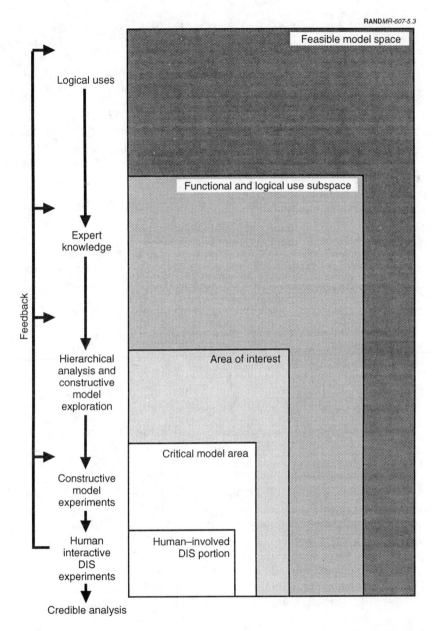

Figure 5.3—An Iterative Approach, Combined with the Proper Experimental
Designs, Provides a Framework for Comprehensive DIS-Supported Analysis

tive modeling is reported by the U.S. Air Force.[32] Here interactive simulator runs were used to identify differences between pilot tactics in the simulators and the constructive models. The models were then adjusted to more accurately reflect the risk-averse decisionmaking seen by the participants in the interactive runs, but not previously incorporated by the models.

Of course, information gleaned at one level of the analysis can and should be fed back to other levels. For example, hypotheses generated in the interactive DIS part may be investigated by additional constructive model runs.

Figure 5.3 is overly simplistic. In reality, the divisions and links between the subspaces are not so clean. However, this figure does illustrate an important concept: Use of expert opinion, logical uses, and complementary constructive analysis, combined with properly designed experiments, can dramatically improve the efficiency and generalizability of DIS-supported studies. In many cases the limitations at the design-of-experiment phase of the credible analysis pyramid may require the analysts to reconsider their logical use. That is, the samples available may not support a given logical use, say formal hypothesis testing, and a less ambitious use must be undertaken.

OTHER DIS STATISTICAL ANALYSIS ISSUES

There are a few other design issues concerning DIS that deserve some comment, such as reproducibility and human elements. These two are interrelated in that much of the difficulty associated with reproduction results from human elements. Having humans in the loop adds variability that must be accounted for in analysis. This includes variations between the participants (i.e., in statistical terms this is random effects modeling) and learning effects within the participants.

It takes many samples to reasonably estimate effects in models containing random elements. Because of the expense and logistics involved with human participation, it is likely that participants in

---

[32]See AF/XOM (1994).

studies will be used in repeated trials. Any analysis study that wants to generalize its results must be designed with participant learning effects in mind. For example, if a DIS-based study with a fixed set of human participants is comparing the effectiveness of two systems, it must not take all of the replications of one system prior to the other; otherwise, learning among the players will likely bias the results.[33] In this case, the systems' effectiveness would be confounded with the learning effects. To mitigate learning effects related to a specific scenario, one may want to randomly and dynamically change the platforms that the human participants represent in different replications. For example, one could randomly assign the human participants to elements that used SAFORs in previous runs. A more ambitious approach would be to attempt to incorporate learning effects explicitly within the analysis.

The participants in DIS studies are likely to be a sample from a larger population. For example, the participants in simulators may be a sample from a larger population. Say the participants are, or are assumed to be, a sample from the population of F-15E pilots. If the sample is not taken randomly from the target population, one has to be very careful about how one generalizes results. For instance, if the F-15E simulator participants are not field pilots, but stationed at the simulator facility, then any conclusions must be qualified with this fact. Additionally, the variability among the participants is likely to increase the overall variability of the outcomes. In statistical terms, the pilots are a random effect. As such, testing for differences among pilots and interactions between pilots and other effects can be more difficult. For more on this, see Montgomery (1991).

One of the fundamental principles of experimental design is repeatability (Kempthorne (1952)). Replication is needed, at a minimum, to estimate variability and test for statistical significance. More important, exact reproducibility is essential for tracing and testing causal relations within a simulation environment. In particular, one must be able to determine whether key causal elements are functions of real phenomena or simply modeling artifacts. An analyst must be able to exactly replicate and selectively modify previous

---

[33]This concern is specifically stated for effectiveness analysis. For other uses, such as training or human/machine interface studies, learning effects may not be deleterious to the experiment.

runs in order to track down and verify the causes of unexpected phenomena.

With constructive simulations, reproducibility can be relatively simple. One simply needs to record all initial conditions, including random number seeds. In principle, one can do something similar with DIS trials by logging all the data, including all human actions that affect outcomes. To replicate things exactly, the timing of events and messages must be kept both internally within a simulation, to control its own event timing, and externally, to control when it communicates to other simulations. This will allow an analyst to replay and examine any level of detail desired. One difficulty of this approach is that if analysts, upon hypothesizing a causal element, want to test the hypothesis by running in-progress excursions, they will be encumbered by human factors. For instance, human learning may make the subsequent excursions not independent of the previous runs.[34]

----

[34]For instance, if a pilot in a helicopter simulation got shot down after going around a hill, he may now use a different flight path, thereby confounding in-progress modifications with his learned behavior.

Chapter Six

CONCLUSIONS

TYPOLOGY OF LOGICAL USES AND ASSOCIATED CREDIBILITY CRITERIA

In this report we have described a typology of categories of logical uses for DIS and defined criteria for determining each use's credibility. This typology is displayed again in Figure 6.1. The typology first distinguishes between using DIS as an experiential stimulus and as an analytic aid.

Assessments of credibility for experiential uses of DIS must be based upon testing of the individual participants to see if they have the desired experience. The means for doing this varies with the nature of the experience. In training for standardized proficiencies where there is strong transferability, there are completely objective means for testing. When training for standardized proficiencies that are only weakly transferable, there are objective criteria, but nonobjective means are required to assess whether they are being met. For those experiential uses where there are no standards, assessments of credibility will require subjective judgment on the part of appropriate experts.

Assessing the credibility of DIS as an analytic aid depends upon the degree of predictivity required of the system for that use. Nonpredictive uses require little predictive power from DIS. Hence, for these uses credibility depends on the verification that the system performs the logical functions expected of it. Strongly predictive uses treat system outputs as detailed predictions of expected real-world outcomes. For these uses, credibility requires statistically rig-

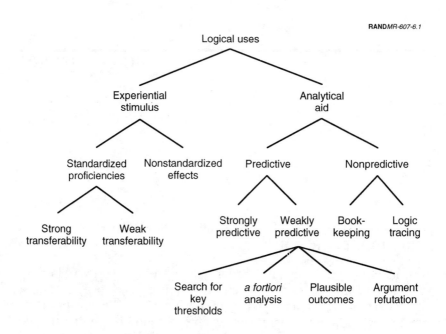

RANDMR-607-6.1

Figure 6.1—Typology of Logical Uses of DIS

orous model validation. Between these extremes is a large class of uses that require weak predictivity. For these uses, credibility depends not only on system characteristics, but on the details of the intended analytic argument and associated research strategy.

VERIFICATION, VALIDATION, ACCREDITATION, AND CREDIBILITY

In the past, the credibility of simulation-based applications has been assessed through a process of verification, validation, and accreditation (VV&A). While all three of these activities are clearly needed in the context of DIS, their relative importance varies significantly across the categories of logical use. For nonpredictive analysis, credibility can be established by means of verification. For strongly predictive analysis and experiential uses that have strongly transferable standardized proficiencies, there are means to validate the system or training protocol, and this validation is necessary and sufficient to establish credible use. For weakly predictive analysis and experiential uses that are either nonstandardized or weakly transferable, subjective judgment is unavoidable in assessing credibility. Consequently, it is for these uses that a formalized process of accreditation is most needed.

IMPLICATIONS FOR THE DESIGN OF DIS

The approach to determining credible uses of DIS that is espoused in this report has several implications for the design of DIS.

Across the DIS community there is a diversity of opinions on how DIS should properly be thought of, and how it should be defined. At one extreme, any constructive model made available for distributed use over DSI is considered to be a part of DIS. At the other, DIS is often envisioned as a "one size fits all" seamless virtual battlefield. In sorting out these different perspectives, it must be recognized that decisions made about the design of DIS will have impacts on the credible uses of DIS. The DIS vision of a seamless virtual battlefield captures much of what is novel and exciting about the approach. However, to the extent that this vision leads developers to pursue a goal of a single "ideal" representation, it will severely limit the number of credible uses for DIS. As we have noted, many applications will have individual realism requirements, including purposeful unrealism. The most useful DIS system will be one that allows customization on a per-application basis.

We have argued that multiple uses for DIS imply variable requirements for realism and multiple criteria for establishing credibility or validity. It has at times been assumed that DIS will eventually be a seamless virtual battlefield, which will serve a variety of needs. Our approach suggests that the greatest utility of DIS for analysis can only be achieved if DIS can support a variety of alternative battlefields, including those tailored for a particular study. This suggests that DIS should not be thought of as a model. Rather, it is a medium that supports modeling, and other uses as well.

SOME NUMERICAL CONSIDERATIONS IN EXPERIMENTAL DESIGN

This appendix provides a table (Table A.1) that compares the number of samples required in a few different designs and summarizes the strength of the conclusions that can be made from them. This example considers a simple case in which only two levels are required on each of 100 variables; yet it illustrates the power of this general approach to partitioning the variables into the above classes. For this example, given the logical use, it is assumed that there are three variables of primary interest, with seven others that the researcher thinks might have some practical influence on outcomes. The seven variables are believed to affect the output in the same direction, if at all, and are thus placed into one group. The remaining 90 variables are strongly believed, but not absolutely known, to be insignificant in the area of interest—a belief the credible argument requires to be substantiated.

Table A.1

Minimum Sample Sizes Required by Design Type to Study a 100-Variable Model, Each Variable Containing Exactly Two Levels

Design	Number of Samples	Summary of Design Strengths and Weaknesses
Full factorial	$n \times 2^{100} \cong n \times 10^{30}$	All main effects and interactions are estimable.
Main effects design	$n \times 100$	All main effects are estimable, but confounded with interactions.
Full factorial on critical variables, crossed with grouped screened variables, and others perturbed 10 times	$n \times (3^2 \times 2) + 10 = 18n + 10$	All critical main effects and their interactions are estimable, including interactions with the grouped screen variables. Screened variable main effects and interactions are all confounded. General stability of outputs to perturbations is established.
Full factorial on critical variables, not crossed with grouped screened variables, and others perturbed 10 times	$n \times (3^2 + 2) + 10 = 11n + 10$	All critical variable main effects and their interactions are estimable, interactions with the grouped screened variables are not estimable. Screened variable group main effect is estimable. General stability of outputs to perturbations is established.
Full factorial on critical variables, and all others perturbed 10 times	$n \times (3^2) + 10 = 9n + 10$	All critical variables and their interactions are estimable. General stability of outputs to screened and perturbation variables is established.

NOTES: It is assumed there are three critical variables and seven screen variables, all grouped together. There are n replications for each case.

AF/XOM, "Connecting Simulation Capabilities in the TBA," *Issues in Air Force Simulation and Analysis,* August 1994.

Atkinson, A. C., and V. V. Fedorov, "Optimum Design of Experiments," *Encyclopedia of Statistical Sciences: Supplement Volume,* New York: Wiley, 1989, pp. 107–114.

Bankes, S. C., "Exploratory Modeling for Policy Analysis," *Operations Research,* Vol. 41, No. 3, May–June 1993.

————, *Issues in Developing the Potential of Distributed Warfare Simulation,* Santa Monica, CA: RAND, R-4131-DARPA, 1992.

Box, G. E. P., and N. R. Draper, *Empirical Model-Building and Response Surfaces,* New York: Wiley, 1987.

Burdick, C. D., "Seamless Simulation: Mixing Live and Virtual Simulation," *Proceedings of the Winter Simulation Conference,* San Diego: Society for Computer Simulation, 1993.

Cochran, W. G., and G. M. Cox, *Experimental Designs,* 2d ed., New York: Wiley, 1957.

Davis, P. K., *Generalizing Concepts and Methods of Verification, Validation, and Accreditation (VV&A) for Military Simulations,* Santa Monica, CA: RAND, R-4249-ACQ, 1992.

———— (ed.), *New Challenges for Defense Planning: Rethinking How Much Is Enough,* Santa Monica, CA: RAND, MR-400-RC, 1994.

Davis, P. K., and D. Blumenthal, *The Base-of-Sand Problem: A White Paper on the State of Military Combat Modeling,* Santa Monica, CA: RAND, N-3148-OSD/DARPA, 1991.

Davis, P. K., and R. Hillestad, "Families of Models That Cross Levels of Resolution: Issues for Design, Calibration, and Management," *Proceedings of the Winter Simulation Conference,* San Diego: Society for Computer Simulation, 1993.

Davis, P. K., and R. K. Huber, *Variable-Resolution Combat Modeling: Motivations, Issues, and Principles,* Santa Monica, CA: RAND, N-3400-DARPA, 1992.

Defense Modeling and Simulation Office (DMSO), *Modeling and Simulation (M&S) Master Plan* (Draft), Washington, D.C.: Office of the Under Secretary of Defense for Acquisition and Technology, DoD 5000.59-P, January 1995.

Defense Science Board, *Computer Applications to Training and Wargaming,* Washington, D.C.: Office of the Under Secretary of Defense for Acquisition, 1988.

———, *Impact of Advanced Distributed Simulation On Readiness, Training, and Prototyping,* Washington, D.C.: Office of the Under Secretary of Defense for Acquisition, 1993.

———, *Report of the Defense Science Board Task Force on Advanced Distributed Simulation,* Office of the Under Secretary of Defense for Acquisition and Technology, 1992.

Department of the Army, *Verification, Validation, and Accreditation of Army Models and Simulation,* Department of the Army Pamphlet 5-11, July 22, 1993.

———, *Distributed Interactive Simulation (DIS) Master Plan 1994* (Draft), Washington, D.C.: Department of the Army, 1994.

Dewar, J. A., J. J. Gillogly, and M. L. Juncosa, *Non-Monotonicity, Chaos and Combat Models,* Santa Monica, CA: RAND, R-3995-RC, 1991.

Dorfman, R., "The Detection of Defective Members of Large Populations," *Annals of Mathematical Statistics,* Vol. 14, 1943, pp. 436–440.

Dubon, L. P., "Joining a Distributed Environment Via ALSP," *Proceedings of the Winter Simulation Conference,* San Diego: Society for Computer Simulation, 1993.

Guckenberger, D., et al., *Teaching High-Performance Skills Using Above-Real-Time Training,* NASA Contractor Report 4528, 1993.

Harshberger, T., "Connecting Simulation Capabilities in the TBA," *Issues in Air Force Simulation and Analysis,* August 1994.

Hillestad, R. J., R. Huber, and M. G. Weiner (eds.), *New Issues and Tools for Future Military Analysis: A Workshop Summary,* Santa Monica, CA: RAND, N-3403-DARPA/AF/A, 1992.

Hodges, J. S., and J. A. Dewar, *Is It You or Your Model Talking? A Framework for Model Validation,* Santa Monica, CA: RAND, R-4114-A/AF/OSD, 1992.

Hoeber, F. P., "Military Applications of Modeling: Selected Case Studies," *Military Operations Research,* 1981.

Hofer, R., and M. Loper, "DIS Today," *Proceedings of the IEEE,* Vol. 83, No. 8, August 1995.

Institute for Simulation and Training (IST), *The DIS Vision: A Map to the Future of Distributed Simulation,* Version 1, Orlando: University of Central Florida, May 1994.

Kempthorne, O., *The Design and Analysis of Experiments,* New York: Wiley, 1952.

Kotz, S., and N. L. Johnson, "Dorfman-Type Screening Procedures," *Encyclopedia of Statistical Sciences: Supplement Volume,* New York: Wiley, 1989, pp. 50–53.

Lewis, Robert O., *A Paradigm for VV&A of Models and Simulations Used in Distributed Interactive Simulation (DIS) Environments,* 1994.

McLean, R. A., and V. L. Anderson, *Applied Factorial and Fractional Designs*, Marcel Dekker, 1984.

Meidt, G. J., and K. W. Bauer, "PCRSM: A Decision Support System for Simulation Metamodel Construction," *Simulation*, Vol. 59, No. 3, 1992, pp. 183–191.

Miller, D., and J. Thorpe, "The Advent of Simulator Networking," *Proceedings of the IEEE*, Vol. 83, No. 8, August 1995.

Montgomery, D. C., *Design and Analysis of Experiments*, New York: Wiley, 1991.

Murphy, A. H., and R. L. Winkler, "Reliability of Subjective Probability Forecasts of Precipitation and Temperature," *Applied Statistics*, Vol. 26, 1974, pp. 41–47.

Office of Technology Assessment, *Virtual Reality and Technologies for Combat Simulation*, Washington D.C.: Office of Technology Assessment, Congress of the United States, 1994.

Padmos, P., "Visual Modeling Errors in the Leopard 2 Driving Simulator," Soesterberg: IZF, IZF-TNO Report, 1986.

Quade, E. S. (ed.), *Analysis for Military Decisions: The RAND Lectures on Systems Analysis*, Chicago: Rand McNally and North Holland, 1964.

Quade, E. S., and W.I. Boucher, *Systems Analysis and Policy Planning: Applications in Defense*, New York: American Elsevier Publishing Co., 1968.

Rolph, J. E., and D. L. Steffey, *Statistical Issues in Defense Analysis and Testing: Summary of a Workshop*, Washington, D.C.: National Academy Press, 1994.

Sanders, A. F., "Simulation as a Tool in the Measurement of Human Performance," *Ergonomics*, Vol. 34, No. 8, 1991.

Sandmeyer, R.S., "Simtech Project: Application of Supercomputers to Division/Corps Level Combat Simulation," AMSAA, Interim Note No. C-159, October 1990.

Shifflett, J., and D. Lunceford, "DoD Applications of DIS," *Proceedings of the IEEE,* Vol. 83, No. 8, August 1995.

Smith, F. R., and R. M. West, *Expanded Test Report—Line-of-Sight Antitank (LOSAT) System,* USA TEXCOM, 92-CT-01082, September 1992.

Sobel, M., and R. M. Elashoff, "Group Testing With a New Goal, Estimation," *Biometrika,* Vol. 62, 1975, pp. 181–193.

Taguchi, G., "An Introduction to Quality Control," Nagoya, Japan: Central Quality Control Association, 1976.

Thomas, C. J., "Models and Wartime Combat Operations Research," in W. P. Hughes (ed.), *Military Modeling,* 2d ed., Alexandria, VA: Military Operations Research Society, 1989.

Torre, J. P., Jr., J. L. Maxey, Sr., and S. Piper, "A Validation of a Rifle Marksmanship Simulation," *Proceedings of the 1988 Summer Computer Simulation Conference,* IEEE, July 1988, pp. 653–657.

TRAC-WSMR, *Results of the M1A2 SIMNET-D Synthetic Environment Post-Experiment Analysis,* White Sands Missile Range, NM, May 1993.